SARCOPHAGUS

VLADIMIR GUBARYEV

SARCOPHAGUS

A TRAGEDY

**Translated from the Russian
by Michael Glenny**

**Preface by
Robert Peter Gale, M.D., Ph.D.**

**VINTAGE BOOKS
A Division of Random House
New York**

FIRST VINTAGE BOOKS EDITION, September 1987

Library of Congress Cataloging-in-Publication Data
Gubaryev, Vladimir.
Sarcophagus: a tragedy.
Translation of: Sarkofag. Originally
published in "Znamia," no. 9, 1986.
1. Nuclear power plants—Ukraine—
Chernobyl—Accidents—Drama.
I. Znamia. II. Title.
PG3481.6.U225S2713 1987   891.72'44   87-40112
ISBN 0-394-75590-1 (pbk.)

TEXT DESIGN BY TASHA HALL

Manufactured in the United States of America
10 9 8 7 6 5 4 3 2 1

PREFACE

On April 26, 1986, Chernobyl exploded onto the world scene. Chernobyl was the site of the world's most serious nuclear accident, for in a few hours its reactors had released a cloud of radioactivity that encircled the globe and affected the lives of millions of people.

It is now a little more than one year later, yet Chernobyl continues to attract worldwide attention. Why? The answer is complex, but important factors include increased interest in and debate about the effects of nuclear energy, its health implications, the future of nuclear power, and increasing concern over nuclear weapons and the prospect of nuclear war.

But there is something more profound about Chernobyl, because what it really represents is civilization's first encounter with the mystery and power of the atom. True, the nuclear age had other beginnings—Enrico Fermi's work in his laboratory under a football field at the University of Chicago and, of course, the atomic bomb explosions over Hiroshima and Nagasaki were historic events that left an indelible mark. But for most people, they were abstract—removed from daily life, from common concerns. Events that did not create the need for moral self-examination, they could be seen as scientific experiments, or as retribution for the attack on Pearl Harbor (thus saving lives through an early end to the war).

Chernobyl changed these perceptions. Suddenly mothers in the United States—10,000 miles from the Soviet Union—wondered if it was safe to give fresh vegetables to their children. People were afraid to travel to Europe after the Chernobyl accident; some remain so. In Europe, the impact of Chernobyl was even more dramatic, and it continues to be a frequent topic of concern and conversation. In the Soviet Union, more than 100,000 people were evacuated from their homes, and most will never return—Pripyat, a large city, stands deserted, perhaps for eternity. Polish parents gave their children iodine tablets; Italians could not eat fresh fruit for several months; Laplanders destroyed their contaminated reindeer, forever changing a major part of their 1,000-year-old culture. All this occurred while a radioactive cloud encircled the planet. Simply put, this is because a nuclear accident anywhere is a nuclear accident *everywhere*. For example, increased incidences of cancer and birth and genetic defects have been predicted for the future—and over one-half of these cases will occur outside of the Soviet Union.

So now we begin to understand the nuclear age—an age we have in for more than forty years—on a personal basis. We also begin to understand the potential consequences of nuclear war. A Welsh farmer whose land is now contaminated recently told me that when he was in the Pacific as a soldier in World War II, he was glad the United States had used the atomic bomb to end the war. Now he's not so sure.

In my opinion, most people—including many scientists, politicians, and military strategists—have little real understanding of the potential consequences of even a limited nuclear exchange. First, the immediate loss of life. Next, contamination of large areas of the planet for hundreds of years and the disruption of the world economy and societal structure as we now know them. Other long-term consequences more difficult to predict accurately include destruction of the earth's protective ozone layer and nuclear winter. One U.S. military strategist not long ago stated that we could survive a nuclear war if we had enough shovels to dig shelters. After Chernobyl, can anyone believe him?

Vladimir Gubaryev has written an interesting play about the Chernobyl accident. It is titled *Sarcophagus*, named for the 300,000-ton concrete-and-steel structure that entombs the reactor core. The word "sarcophagus" recalls ancient mummified Egyptian monarchs—silent, still, nonbreathing. But what of the modern sarcophagus? It entombs a modern-day pharaoh, a pharaoh still alive, and one that will remain so beyond the lifetimes of all those who read these lines.

In some ways, the implications of Chernobyl are too great, too disturbing, to be contemplated voluntarily. Gubaryev humanizes them. He dramatizes the medical activities that immediately followed the accident, events in which my Soviet colleagues and I played active roles.

It is not important if the details of *Sarcophagus* are not precise. Angelina Guskova—the actual doctor that the character of Ptitsyna is based on—tells me that she is not as old in body or mind as depicted, and I, unfortunately, am not a millionaire; perhaps Kyle is a chimera of Hammer and Gale. But what *Sarcophagus* does do is deal with the profound implications of Chernobyl on a personal level: life and death, victim and healer, hero and coward. *Sarcophagus* is also surprisingly honest—perhaps because of the spirit of *glasnost*, or the seriousness of the subject.

After reading or viewing this play, many people will find themselves thinking about the dangers of nuclear energy. But what conclusions should be drawn? Clearly, technologies are not inherently good or evil; society determines their role. And so it is with nuclear energy. Radiation is used successfully to cure children suffering from cancer, but it is also used to make nuclear weapons that can end life. We, not nuclear energy, will determine whether that energy will be used for good or for evil. In an earlier time, I could have added, "and history will record the decision." But we have moved to a new era: if we misuse nuclear energy, there will be no history.

I am an optimist; I have faith in people, in our society. I believe we will find a way out of the dilemmas posed by nuclear energy. Paradoxically, this process may even have been helped by what happened at Chernobyl. How? By heightening public awareness; by emphasizing the interdependence of all of us who inhabit this small planet; by showing the Soviets that Americans, in giving aid, hold the value of life above political differences; and by showing that science and medicine know no boundaries. *Sarcophagus* is one small but important step in this process. As stated earlier, nuclear energy anywhere on this planet is nuclear energy everywhere. We are all in it together, so we had better find ways to work together, or we may all perish. To paraphrase Albert Einstein, the survival of mankind will depend on developing an entirely new manner of thinking about the promise and danger of nuclear energy.

ROBERT PETER GALE, M.D., PH.D.
*University of California, Los Angeles,
and Armand Hammer Center
for Advanced Studies in
Nuclear Energy and Health*

FOREWORD

"There is no concealing the fact: there are people who think it is time to forget about Chernobyl on the grounds that more important matters are claiming our attention, and anyway . . . 'Why must we constantly harp on this tragedy?' Worse still, there are also people who are trying to cover up the truth about Chernobyl—indeed, to lie about it. Lies, however, are needed only by those who can't do their jobs properly, who need to hide their own incompetence and cowardice. There is only one way of avoiding a repetition of Chernobyl: to tell the truth about what happened, to make the most painstaking analysis of the causes of the tragedy—and not to let the culprits get away with it. For only the cleansing truth will show us the way into the future . . ."

Although published as part of a review of a television documentary on Chernobyl, this paragraph, written by Vladimir Gubaryev in his role of Science Editor of *Pravda*, could equally well serve as a succinct account of the motivation behind *Sarcophagus*—the play that he has written in his capacity as a spare-time dramatist.

Wearing his journalist's hat, Gubaryev was the first reporter on the spot following the disastrous accident at No. 4 Reactor of the Chernobyl nuclear power station, to which he was sent by his editor-in-chief to cover the immediate aftermath of the explosion in late April and early May 1986. From there he filed a series of reports for *Pravda*, which gave readers as much information as was then known about the causes of the explosion and its effects on those who were unfortunate enough to be its victims. He had, however, also been commissioned to write a longer piece, more analytical and more reflective, for publication in *Znamya* (the "Banner"), a monthly literary journal that is part of the *Pravda* publishing enterprise.

Rather to his own surprise, Gubaryev found that the strength of feeling aroused in him when witnessing the consequences of the accident—and, above all, when talking to the survivors, many of whom were doomed to an early death from radiation sickness—was too great to be expressed in the sober prose customary in the news columns of a national daily newspaper. Convinced that the only medium adequately able to convey his thoughts and emotions on this truly terrible subject was the theater, with its unique power of direct, instantaneous communication across the narrow gap between stage and auditorium, Gubaryev decided not to write a conventional article for *Znamya*. Instead he put his observations, his feelings and his reactions to Chernobyl into a play, in the hope that it would be noticed by theater directors and given exposure to an audience wider than the readership of *Znamya* (although, with an average print run of 250,000 copies, this journal has a circulation that would make the editorial boards of most English-language literary magazines faint with envy). He finished writing the play on July 5, 1986, and it was published in the September 1986 issue of *Znamya*.

To achieve this, a story already earmarked to appear in that issue was taken out at proof stage and its publication postponed, such was the importance accorded to *Sarcophagus*. The play's rapid appearance in print is fast by Western standards, but in the Soviet Union, where until very recently the time lag between acceptance of a manuscript and its publication in a literary magazine could be as much as a year, it is quite phenomenal. This, taken in conjunction with the striking fact that a work containing so much critical subject matter is being published at all, is evidence of the urgency that was given to the play's publication by the Soviet leadership—and in all probability, by Gorbachev himself—because without significant pressure from the very top the hitherto bureaucratic process of discussion, censorship, approval and publication could not have been speeded up to such a remarkable degree.

Sarcophagus is not only a thought-provoking play about a burning issue of the day; in the long run it will probably be seen as of equal significance in having marked a highly visible turning-point in the relationship between the Communist Party of the Soviet Union and the media, in particular where the proscriptive control of information is concerned. Until Gorbachev came to power, all Soviet media, without exception, were forbidden to mention such things as crime, prison camps, labor disputes, epidemics, natural disasters and manmade disasters such as major industrial accidents, train wrecks and airplane crashes occurring within the Soviet Union and its immediate sphere of influence. The reason behind these wide-ranging prohibitions was a part of the obscure, often irrational and ultimately counterproductive measures of censorship that originated under Stalin and have been kept in force until recently. One of Gorbachev's most remarkable moves in his campaign for *glasnost* or openness in Soviet public life has been largely to abolish these taboos on giving information to the Soviet public at large. *Sarcophagus* is one of the first fruits of this policy, while the Chernobyl disaster itself was to a great extent the irresistible force that obliged the hitherto immovable block of Soviet news censorship to give way, if only because the effects of nuclear fall-out from Chernobyl were felt all over Europe and could not effectively be concealed from the Soviet people.

While this play is notable for the freedom with which authors may handle subject matter of a kind that is now being given a public airing for the first time, it is as well to point out that there are matters that Gubaryev has chosen *not* to deal with, and there are approaches to his topic that he has consciously avoided. First, in explaining the causes of the Chernobyl accident, he was obviously unable to go beyond the information that was available to him at the time of writing; he could not, for instance, use the data that became generally known after the Soviet delegation had delivered its very full report to the International Atomic Energy Agency in Vienna in October 1986, because it had not yet been collated and analyzed. We therefore know considerably more of these facts now than did Gubaryev in June 1986, although such technical information that is given in the play is wholly consistent with our subsequent, more detailed knowledge. Secondly, *Sarcophagus* is not a polemic against the use of civil nuclear energy. Although fueled by a considerable charge of emotion, the author has not set out to be a partisan on either side of that issue but rather to stress what he sees as the appalling dangers inherent in the way that this energy source has so far been handled by those responsible for it. These are the facts, he is saying: disregard them at your peril. Possessed of these facts, it is then the business of the politicians, their scientists, the administrators and ultimately the public to debate and to pronounce on the broader questions raised by the play's warning.

In devising a theatrical format to put that warning across to the audience, Gubaryev has avoided the technical jargon-mongering, mechanical gimmickry or contrived horrors of the science-fiction school of writing. Yet the gravity of the disaster is not shirked or concealed; the author's method of tackling this technically (and politically) daunting subject is to focus our attention primarily on its human aspect, namely, the experiences and reactions of a small group of people immediately affected—whether as victims or as medical personnel—by the dreadful physical and psychological consequences for human beings of massive doses of radiation. Within this context we learn about the causes of the disaster and its wider implications, sometimes obliquely, from the dialogue. Not all is left to inference, however; two of the characters are very senior officials in responsible positions, and when these men are interrogated by an investigator from the State Prosecutor's office, it is then that the author hits hardest at the culprits.

In writing *Sarcophagus* Gubaryev has not only chosen the form of naturalistic drama; he has written a piece that keeps very closely to the Aristotelian canons of Greek tragedy: the unities of time, place and action are strictly observed; violent events take place offstage and are reported to us; death, though ever-present, occurs out of our sight; and the underlying message is that through hubris (in this case by failing lamentably to treat the great god Atom with proper respect) we bring nemesis upon ourselves. In a moment of sardonic prophecy the play's central character looks forward into the distant future and—assuming that the human race has survived for so long—he indicts the people responsible for the Chernobyl disaster:

Just imagine: none of us will be here then, not even our great-great-great-grandchildren. All our cities will have gone . . . even the pyramids of Egypt will be just a handful of dust—yet the sarcophagus around this reactor of yours will still be standing. The pyramids of the Pharaohs have been there for a mere five thousand years. But to contain the radiation, your nuclear pyramid must remain for at least a hundred thousand years ... That's some monument to leave to our descendants, isn't it?

MICHAEL GLENNY
March 1987

SARCOPHAGUS

CHARACTERS

LYDIA STEPANOVNA PTITSYNA	Professor of Surgery
ANNA PETROVNA	Physician and research scientist
LEV IVANOVICH SERGEYEV	Medical Director, Institute of Radiation Safety
VERA NADEZHDA LYUBOV	Newly qualified doctors
INVESTIGATOR	Official of State Prosecutor's Department
KYLE	American Professor of Surgery
CYCLIST	(Cubicle No. 1)
KLAVA	(Cubicle No. 2)
FIREMAN	(Cubicle No. 3)
DRIVER	(Cubicle No. 4)
DIRECTOR OF NUCLEAR POWER STATION	(Cubicle No. 5) Patients
GEIGER-COUNTER OPERATOR	(Cubicle No. 6)
CONTROL-ROOM OPERATIVE	(Cubicle No. 7)
GENERAL	(Cubicle No. 8)
PHYSICIST	(Cubicle No. 9)
BESSMERTNY, alias KROLIK	(Cubicle No. 10)
ORDERLIES	

The action takes place, unfortunately, in the present day.

The American premiere of the play took place at the Los Angeles Theatre Center (artistic producing director, Bill Bushnell; producer, Diane White) on September 17, 1987, with the following cast:

LYDIA STEPANOVNA PTITSYNA	Nan Martin
ANNA PETROVNA	Barbara Tarbuck
LEV IVANOVICH SERGEYEV	Robert Symonds
VERA (FAITH)	Patrice Martinez
NADEZHDA (HOPE)	Erin Cressida Wilson
LYUBOV (CHARITY)	Penny Johnson
INVESTIGATOR	Aled Davies
KYLE	Brian Brophy
CYCLIST	Jere Burns
KLAVA	Nobu McCarthy
FIREMAN	John Cameron Mitchell
DRIVER	E. J. Castillo
DIRECTOR OF NUCLEAR POWER STATION	Ben Piazza
GEIGER-COUNTER OPERATIVE	Daniel Roebuck
CONTROL-ROOM OPERATIVE	Henry G. Sanders
FIRE MARSHAL (GENERAL)	Tom Rosqui
PHYSICIST	Alan Mandell
BESSMERTNY, alias KROLIK	Gregory Wagowski
ORDERLIES	Scott Wilder
	Joseph Keeper
	Linda Browne

Directed by Bill Bushnell
Produced by Diane White
Set, lighting, and costume design by Timian Alsaker
Sound by Jon Gottlieb
Makeup design by Robert Scribner and Stacey Zimmerman
Stage manager: Jill Johnson

ACT ONE

The medical experimental section of the Institute of Radiation Safety. A large hall, furnished center-stage with comfortable arm-chairs and a few low tables—the section's daily morning conferences are held here. Stage right, behind a glass screen, is the desk of the Duty Physician; on it are a telephone under a locked Plexiglas cover and a lamp. At the rear of the set is a row of cubicles with frosted-glass doors, numbered 1 to 10 from left to right; behind them is a cyclorama.

SCENE ONE

The light is on in Cubicle No. 10; the rest are dark. BESSMERTNY *comes out of No. 10, looks around, tiptoes over to the Duty Physician's desk. He tries to open the Plexiglas cover over the telephone but cannot do so because it is locked. Enter* ANNA PETROVNA, *who watches* BESSMERTNY.

ANNA PETROVNA: I've got the key. Anyhow, who is there for you to call?

BESSMERTNY: The longing just got the better of me . . . Who can I call? Any number, just to hear a human voice. It's so deadly all on one's own . . . But why are you back from your vacation, Anna Petrovna? By my reckoning, you still have another three days' leave to go.

ANNA PETROVNA: Sergeyev asked me to come back early. There's a conference in two weeks, and he's giving a paper. (*Crosses the hall and sinks down in an armchair.*) There's nothing more exhausting than being on vacation.

BESSMERTNY: I told you to go south, to a sanatorium. You can't relax properly at your own dacha. All those flower-beds to dig, carrots and all that, the cherry trees . . .

ANNA PETROVNA: The cherry trees aren't out for another three weeks yet.

BESSMERTNY: Anyway, there are always chores to do. I've never had a dacha of my own, mind you, but I imagine . . . I have been down south, though—to Alupka. . . . Used to get a free travel warrant from the union . . . That was about ten years ago now, but I'll always remember those holidays in the south. I never actually went bathing. Too cold for it—it was in either December or January, I forget which—but I longed to take a dip all the same. One day the lads and I got warmed up on a few drinks and we all went down to the beach, started getting undressed and just then the Frontier Guards . . .

ANNA PETROVNA: *Frontier Guards?* In Alupka?

BESSMERTNY: Don't they have them there? Oh, well, then it was the police. Anyway, they wouldn't let us go in the water. It was a pity. In all my life I've never yet managed to swim in the sea. By the way, I'm glad you're back from leave. While you were away we had nothing but temporary

Duty Officers, and they're all scared stiff of coming in here. I tried to convince them, but it was a waste of time. They're frightened of me, as if I were a leper.

ANNA PETROVNA: I see you've moved into No. 10.

BESSMERTNY: I got bored with the one I was in before. I'll stay in No. 10 for a while, then move to No. 5. At least it's in the middle. Or should I start again in No. 1?

ANNA PETROVNA: Please yourself. . . . Oh yes, I've been collecting crosswords for you. I cut them out of all the newspapers. (*Hands him a bunch of clippings.*)

BESSMERTNY: So you didn't forget. Thanks very much. . . . I've been so bored without you. It really means something to have someone intelligent to talk to.

ANNA PETROVNA: Some new interns arrived today. Newly qualified young doctors who are going to work at nuclear power stations. If you've no objection, I'll introduce you to them.

BESSMERTNY: Can I refuse you anything, Anna Petrovna? Your wish is my command. If it's in the cause of medical science, I'm at your service.

(ANNA PETROVNA *gets up, goes over to the Duty Physician's desk, unlocks the cover on the telephone and dials a number.*)

ANNA PETROVNA: (*After slight pause, into the receiver*) Hello. Yes. Yes, we're expecting them. . . . Three, is it? . . . Yes, Lydia Stepanovna, I'll give them the usual talk. I know what they need to be told . . . Yes, we're all ready. . . . (*Puts down the receiver.*)

BESSMERTNY: Are they coming?

ANNA PETROVNA: They're in the greenhouse at the moment.

BESSMERTNY: I went there once—on an outing. Professor Sergeyev let me go. The size of the mushrooms they grow there! I suggested they ought to grow a mushroom as big as . . . as big as this room! Big enough to feed an entire family of four, so that from one mushroom you could have soup, main course and enough left over to make mushroom sauce for another day. There was such a sweet . . . well, funny young girl lab assistant there. She said to me: "Have you forgotten about all the strontium and caesium in these mushrooms?" And she laughed. As if *I* would be likely to forget them! So, my dear Anna Petrovna, all you have to do is to discover how to remove the radiation from irradiated fungi and you and I could flood the country with super-mushrooms. How's that for an idea?

ANNA PETROVNA: (*Smiling*) You always did have a vivid imagination.

BESSMERTNY: It's all I have to live for since I've been imprisoned in this place as a guinea pig for your scientific experiments. . . . Excuse me, I hear our visitors coming. I must go and freshen myself up. Make them wait a bit till I'm ready.

(*Exit* BESSMERTNY *into Cubicle No. 10. Enter* VERA, NADEZHDA *and* LYUBOV.)

VERA: (*Looking around inquiringly*) This is where we're supposed to be—I think. . . .

NADEZHDA: It's nice here. Not like downstairs.

ANNA PETROVNA: Ah, come in. We've been expecting you.

LYUBOV: What a strange place.

ANNA PETROVNA: Those are special cubicles for terminal-stage patients.

8

NADEZHDA: But they're empty!

ANNA PETROVNA: Fortunately, yes. At the moment we only have one patient.

VERA: But in that case, why . . . ?

ANNA PETROVNA: When the Institute was founded, they thought the cubicles would contain many more patients than they do. But I want to stress that we're *fortunate* in having very few patients.

LYUBOV: And presumably when you do have them, they don't stay here for long?

ANNA PETROVNA: Usually—yes. But there is one exception. And I want to introduce you to him. . . . (VERA *points to the lighted Cubicle No. 10 and* ANNA PETROVNA *nods.*) Did you like it downstairs?

NADEZHDA: The second floor was awful. And pathetic. Especially the little dogs.

LYUBOV: They looked at you as if they understood what was happening to them.

VERA: Oh, Lyuba, don't . . .

ANNA PETROVNA: It's cruel, of course, but it's essential.

VERA: I'm going to ask to be assigned to the second floor.

LYUBOV: I want to be on the first floor—there are only plants there, and they don't look into your eyes the way the dogs and cats do.

VERA: But at least we can relieve the animals' suffering, even if only a little bit.

NADEZHDA: Still, I want to go with Lyuba.

ANNA PETROVNA: Professor Sergeyev will decide that. Although he listens to individual requests, he makes up his own mind.

LYUBOV: He struck me as a rather gentle, kind man. . . .

(*Enter* BESSMERTNY, *wearing an elegant suit, a white shirt and a blue bow tie.*)

BESSMERTNY: Well, here I am.

ANNA PETROVNA: Words fail me!

BESSMERTNY: Since I changed my name, I've also changed my entire lifestyle, Anna Petrovna.

VERA: Excuse me, but how did you change your name?

BESSMERTNY: Simple! I just changed it. . . . So, ladies, I am entirely at your disposal. Where shall we begin? Perhaps, if our charming Anna Petrovna is agreeable, I'll give you a short introduction to my case, and then I'll gladly answer your questions.

ANNA PETROVNA: I have some work to do. If you need me, I'm in there. (*Goes towards the Duty Physician's desk.*)

BESSMERTNY: Please make yourselves comfortable. Allow me. (*Takes* NADEZHDA *by the elbow. She instinctively shrinks away from his touch.*) Oh, don't be alarmed. I'm no danger to you. Quite the opposite—if anything, *you* are a danger to me. But I have made up my mind to overcome my instinctive fears because I am entirely devoted to science. I am literally a slave to science, and this awareness helps me to overcome the weaknesses to which the human soul and body are prone. . . .

ANNA PETROVNA: Perhaps you could come down to earth a bit and sound a little less high-falutin' . . .

VERA: But why, Comrade . . . ?

BESSMERTNY: Bessmertny. At the moment my surname is Bessmertny. "Immortal." I chose it myself. Sounds properly optimistic, doesn't it?

VERA: Er. yes . . . Of course . . .

NADEZHDA: What was your previous name?

BESSMERTNY: Krolik. In other words, "Rabbit." Yes, "Rabbit." Like the ones you saw on the second floor, only spelled with a capital letter. Do you follow me?

VERA: But why did you choose such . . . well, funny names?

BESSMERTNY: I'm an emotional person. I was once in a furious mood because I had a row with Professor Ptitsyna. She had written only six pages of her dissertation about me, which annoyed me, and I didn't conceal it from her. But now that Professors Sergeyev and Ptitsyna have published three articles about me, I realize that my attitude to her was wrong. She has a job to do. She does appreciate me and doesn't just regard me as a laboratory rabbit. So I decided to call myself "Immortal," but if . . . well, if anything happens to me, then I can adopt my previous name again.

NADEZHDA: (*Confused*) I don't understand a thing!

BESSMERTNY: It's not simple, I agree. So let's begin with my introductory remarks. I could, of course, read them out to you, as they usually do at all decent press conferences—the script is in my cubicle—but I think this kind of meeting calls for a more private, intimate sort of talk, so I shall give you the bits of it that I've learned by heart. . . .

(*The cyclorama begins to glow.*)

I have been here 487 days. That fact in itself is unique in medical history, so you, my dear young ladies, can consider yourselves very lucky. Of course, I'm well aware that my own contribution to such an incredible, almost fantastic, phenomenon is not very significant. The main element, of course, has been the knowledge and skill of Professors Ptitsyna and Sergeyev, not forgetting Anna Petrovna here, but I don't want to underrate my own contribution to science either. After all, I have survived sixteen operations—seven bone-marrow transplants, three lung operations and three on the liver. . . . By the way, Anna Petrovna, there are three or four more to come, aren't there?

ANNA PETROVNA: No more than three, I think.

BESSMERTNY: Thank you. Well, not everyone can withstand sixteen operations. . . . And what has been learned in the course of such a unique—I repeat, unique—experiment? Above all, we still don't know enough about what the human organism is capable of when attacked by radiation sickness—or, please note, by what is usually regarded as the terminal stage of the affliction.

VERA: It's impossible. The organism shouldn't be capable of anything.

BESSMERTNY: I quite agree with you. A person in that condition dies after a few days. But, as you see, I am alive and talking to you. The history of the experimentation on me up to the present day has been described in fourteen articles written by staff members of this Institute, two of which will soon appear in the press. My case has also been reported at three big international conferences, which were attended by our medical director, Professor Lev Ivanovich Sergeyev. One aspect of the experiment has been dealt with in two doctoral dissertations, namely, the specific features that characterized the transplantation and compatibility of my bone marrow. Anna Petrovna is working on a dissertation on my liver. I will be glad to show you the complete list of learned publications on my case, in case you haven't come across them yet.

NADEZHDA: I've read some of them, and I must say I didn't believe them. Does this mean that you are "Patient K."?

BESSMERTNY: Yes. From the initial letter of my previous surname—Krolik.

LYUBOV: But what is your . . . *real* surname?

BESSMERTNY: Let's say I've forgotten it.

ANNA PETROVNA: Don't ask him about that. There are no surnames here. No one is allowed to visit this place.

LYUBOV: I'm sorry. I know that. It just slipped out.

BESSMERTNY: All information about our patients can be obtained by inquiring at the Ministry of Health. That is . . . that is, if there is anyone to inquire about.

VERA: What do you mean?

(*The glow on the cyclorama becomes brighter.*)

BESSMERTNY: There is no one to inquire about me. . . . Oh, it's a very romantic story. (*Growing more animated as he continues*) I was in love, and it was mutual. She was a lovely ash-blonde—I've always had a weakness for blonde girls! But one day she met someone else. Smouldering and dark-haired, the kind you often see on television. And she fell for him, hopelessly. . . . No doubt you will know about this sort of thing?

LYUBOV: It happens.

BESSMERTNY: And that passion destroyed both her and me. I went through agonies. Life became unbearable, and one day, in a fit of madness, I stole a small container of plutonium from the laboratory where I worked—you all know, of course, that plutonium is the most powerful source of radio-activity—and I swallowed it. I wanted to die in such a way that she would always remember me, and my rival would always . . .

ANNA PETROVNA: (*A meaningful cough*) Hm'mm. . . .

BESSMERTNY: Look, Anna Petrovna, since the new campaign against this, er, failing . . . I mean, I can't mention alcohol. . . .

ANNA PETROVNA: You can to them.

BESSMERTNY: But I'm so ashamed. . . . I mean to say—three lovely girls . . . and me an alcoholic. No, I can't.

ANNA PETROVNA: The fact is that this patient of ours was dead drunk and fell asleep alongside some experimental apparatus in a nuclear physics laboratory. Unfortunately, no one noticed him. The experiment lasted about three hours. His total dose of radiation exceeded 600 roentgens. He was brought here unconscious.

BESSMERTNY: That's a very dubious version! I can't argue with you, Anna Petrovna, although I think the story about the blonde and the dark-haired Casanova is highly instructive, and it's our responsibility to educate the younger generation.

VERA: And you haven't left that cubicle for more than a year?

BESSMERTNY: 487 days. Still, I have had three outings—twice to the first floor and once to the second floor. But I can't go beyond the ultraviolet curtain. The body's immune system doesn't reestablish itself. I can't live out there in the world of microbes, which is why anyone who is allowed in here has to pass through the special airlock. But Anna Petrovna hopes . . .

ANNA PETROVNA: There is a lot we still don't know.

VERA: And will it go on like this forever?

ANNA PETROVNA: For the time being.

BESSMERTNY: But I feel fine here.

NADEZHDA: Forgive me, but I find that hard to believe. After all, presumably you have a wife, children, close relations. . . .

BESSMERTNY: I have no past. I have forgotten everything about it. Everything. I'm not aware of having a wife and family. My family is here, around me: Anna Petrovna, the security guards, everyone who works here. Beyond these walls there is nothing. Do you understand? *Nothing!*

ANNA PETROVNA: Calm down. . . . (*To* NADEZHDA) You mustn't ask him about these things.

NADEZHDA: But why not?

ANNA PETROVNA: The only people admitted here are patients whose radiation dose exceeds the terminal level—*greatly* exceeds that level. Consequently, there is only one way out of here. Does that sound cruel? On the contrary, it is humane. Our patients simply *cannot* meet their relatives because they cannot survive in proximity to them. Do you realize what the total dysfunction of the body's immune system means? Not just theoretically but in practice? The slightest scratch—infection. A pimple—infection. Outside the protective ultraviolet screen every micro-organism means death. We even bury them inside the confines of the ultraviolet screen, because their bodies are radioactive.

VERA: Then why all this? (*She points around her.*)

ANNA PETROVNA: In order to find out how to overcome the effects of those lethal 600 roentgens. And he (*pointing to* BESSMERTNY) has taken the first step in that direction. It's thanks to him that we're at last beginning to acquire some understanding. The fact that he is still alive is the miracle that is helping us, even though he has been totally deprived of his past. He had to deprive *himself* of his past life. To an outsider it seems unimaginable.

LYUBOV: And all the other patients?

ANNA PETROVNA: There weren't many of them—only a handful—and they are no longer with us.

BESSMERTNY: Anna Petrovna, which one of these three shall we choose to have here in our section?

ANNA PETROVNA: Which one do you like best?

(*The glow on the cyclorama grows steadily brighter.*)

BESSMERTNY: I can't compel any of them to stay here. Girls, which of you likes solving crosswords?

VERA: If you have no objection, I'll apply to come here.

BESSMERTNY: Thank you, my dear! To be honest, I'm desperately bored here. There's nothing worth watching on television. It's all so banal. I'm a free man, especially in the afternoons; there are staff conferences here in the morning. We can pass the time of day, discuss the latest advances in radiation medicine. . . .

ANNA PETROVNA: Our patient is very well up on that subject. I don't mind admitting I quite often ask him for information.

BESSMERTNY: I researched for her two articles to be included in a medical encyclopedia, and Anna Petrovna tells me they've been accepted.

VERA: (*Smiling*) And who gets the fee?

BESSMERTNY: Oh, I haven't thought about that. Perhaps it'll go to a fund for medical research—what do you think? Or I'll subscribe to a crossword magazine that's published in Czechoslovakia—I hear they include a hundred crosswords in each issue. Crosswords are my passion. You know, we have a vast quantity of different sorts of information in our heads, only they're not systematized. I've invented an elegant system that makes sure the necessary word instantly pops up in our memory. To do this, thousands of millions of neurons have to be lined up in a particular order. That's all! There are people who can multiply or divide six-figure numbers in their heads. So we devise a special table . . .

(*An alarm signal sounds. Red lights flash and sirens are heard in the distance.*)

VERA: Has something happened?

NADEZHDA: What was that?

LYUBOV: Does it mean war? Oh, no!

BESSMERTNY: Don't worry. It's a practice alarm. It happens here every so often.

ANNA PETROVNA: Funny. The civil defense people usually do their training in the morning or on Sundays.

BESSMERTNY: I expect there's a new man in charge and he's showing how keen he is.

(*The telephone rings.*)

ANNA PETROVNA: (*Picking up receiver*) Hello . . . speaking . . . it can't have! Which one? . . . I can't believe it! We thought it was a practice alarm. . . . Yes, all three of them are here. . . . OK! They'll be ready.

(ANNA PETROVNA *slowly walks out of the Duty Room into the hall. Silence. She stares hard at each of the three young interns.*)

There has been an accident at No. 4 Reactor at the nuclear power station. A big fire. Several dozen people have been injured including some with radiation burns. They'll be here in a few minutes. (*Addressing* VERA, NADEZHDA *and* LYUBOV) You are now under our orders. There is protective clothing in the next room. Change quickly and come back here. (*To* BESSMERTNY) You must stay in your cubicle and don't come out until further notice.

VERA: But we . . .

ANNA PETROVNA: Do as you're told. And no arguments.

VERA: But we probably won't be able . . .

ANNA PETROVNA: You will! We've no one else.

(VERA *is about to say something else, but* ANNA PETROVNA *pays no attention to her and goes to the telephone. Exeunt* VERA, NADEZHDA *and* LYUBOV. ANNA PETROVNA *dials a number and speaks.*)

Prepare the radioactivity-screening system. The radiation doses have not been determined yet, so be extra careful. So far there are four of us in the section, but Sergeyev and Ptitsyna will be here soon. And check that the operating theaters are ready. We may have to operate right away. Alarm stage one . . . no, no, it's not war. A nuclear reactor has blown up . . . no, *no!* Not a nuclear explosion—a hydrogen explosion inside the reactor.

(*Enter* VERA, NADEZHDA *and* LYUBOV *wearing special blue overalls.*)

NADEZHDA: We're ready. What do we do now?

ANNA PETROVNA: Wait.

NADEZHDA: And then?

ANNA PETROVNA: Nothing out of the ordinary. If necessary, painkillers, drips, the usual casualty procedures.

BESSMERTNY: (*Cautiously opening the door of his cubicle and looking out*) Eight letters, "Gravestone." I can't think of it. The second letter is "O."

ANNA PETROVNA: Monument.

BESSMERTNY: Of course. That might fit. Funny, I never thought of a gravestone as a monument.

ANNA PETROVNA: Look it up in the dictionary.

BESSMERTNY: Thanks. (*Retreats into his cubicle and shuts the door.*)

VERA: It's upsetting. I feel a bit peculiar.

ANNA PETROVNA: In this job the golden rule is: no emotion. Calm and steady, keep a grip on yourself and remember the characteristic features of radiation sickness. At first sight they seem perfectly healthy, especially if they're not in pain. But then the symptoms appear suddenly. Each cubicle contains all the necessary medication.

(*The red glow flares up more brightly.* SERGEYEV *strides in, followed by two* ORDERLIES *carrying a stretcher, on which lies a man.*)

SERGEYEV: Put him in No. 5. (*To* ANNA PETROVNA) He's unconscious. I gave him first aid. Everything necessary has been done.

(*The light goes on in No. 5. Enter* DRIVER, *in uniform, accompanied by an* ORDERLY.)

Cubicle No. 4.

(*The* ORDERLY *hands a card to* SERGEYEV, *who reads it.*)

DRIVER: My general's out there. Perhaps I should wait for him.

SERGEYEV: How do you feel?

DRIVER: Normal.

SERGEYEV: Any dizziness?

DRIVER: I did feel dizzy for about a minute, but then it stopped. What must I do?

ANNA PETROVNA: Vera, show this comrade into No. 4, please. Let him lie down and rest. And change all his clothes. (*To the* DRIVER) You'll have to spend a little time here with us. We'll examine you in a while.

VERA: This way, please.

(*She takes the* DRIVER *by the arm and leads him into Cubicle No. 4.*)

ANNA PETROVNA: Look of slight irritation on his face. How much did he get?

SERGEYEV: Can't say. He was waiting for his boss—the general in charge of security—at No. 4 Reactor. Waited for three hours. Where he was there were up to 500 roentgens an hour. Still, at least he didn't get out of his car . . . so I can't say exactly. But it's a lot.

NADEZHDA: Why was he there for so long?

SERGEYEV: Waiting for a senior officer, his boss. Orders are orders.

NADEZHDA: But there was a lot of radiation there, wasn't there?

SERGEYEV: Unfortunately, my dear, you can't see it or smell it. And the general's used to being in the thick of things. That's how it is.

NADEZHDA: But . . .

SERGEYEV: Exactly—"but." He just jumped into his big black car and drove straight to the reactor!

LYUBOV: But perhaps he didn't know how dangerous it was.

SERGEYEV: It's his job to know!

(*The door of Cubicle No. 5 opens. Two* ORDERLIES *come out of it, one of them carrying a plastic bag full of clothes. Exeunt.* VERA *comes out of Cubicle No. 4.*)

VERA: He's asleep.

ANNA PETROVNA: Keep an eye on him. When he wakes up, we'll examine him.

SERGEYEV: Surgical intervention is not indicated so far.

ANNA PETROVNA: What is the total number of the injured?

SERGEYEV: About three hundred. Those are the ones who got more than a hundred roentgens. As for those with heavier doses, who are due to come here, I can't yet say exactly. Fifteen were sent to the cancer clinic; some others were put in local clinics . . . I was rather late getting there. For a long time they couldn't work out exactly what had happened, so that's why they didn't notify Moscow right away—in case they gave the wrong information. They were waiting for something. . . .

ANNA PETROVNA: Lev Ivanovich, I hope *you* didn't . . .

SERGEYEV: My dear Anna Petrovna, I know too much about radiation to stick my head into the lion's mouth.

ANNA PETROVNA: Yes—but still. Did you . . . ?

SERGEYEV: I got slightly more than a normal annual dose. By the time we arrived, the radiation situation had become clear.

BESSMERTNY: (*Having overheard them and now sticking his head out of his cubicle*) But what *has* happened?

(*The door of Cubicle No. 4 opens and an* ORDERLY *brings out a plastic bag full of clothes.*)

SERGEYEV: (*To* BESSMERTNY) You, of all people, must be careful. We're still processing most of the patients downstairs at the moment, but when they do come, take care.

BESSMERTNY: I see. Is it something terrible?

SERGEYEV: In our business, unfortunately, whatever happens is terrible.

(*Enter* GENERAL.)

GENERAL: (*Turning around*) I don't need an escort! (*To* SERGEYEV) What is going on here? Isn't anyone allowed to go anywhere on his own? They gave me so many jabs in my ass . . . (*Notices the women*) Pardon my language, but I feel like a pin cushion.

ANNA PETROVNA: I expect you were complaining of pains in the small of the back, weren't you?

GENERAL: I had a bit of pain there, but it stopped. I was expecting to be given a quick examination and then allowed to go.

SERGEYEV: You've heard the order, haven't you?

GENERAL: Yes, our minister was really hot under the collar! I don't know what you said to him. But an order's an order. . . . Is my driver here?

SERGEYEV: Yes.

GENERAL: I'm afraid he caught it too. But nothing serious, I hope?

SERGEYEV: You must go into Cubicle No. 8. The first thing to do is to strip and change. . . .

GENERAL: That little fellow of yours downstairs, the one with curly black hair, said my uniform would have to be destroyed. How ridiculous!

SERGEYEV: Well, the uniform's no problem. (*To* LYUBOV) Take the comrade general to his cubicle, please. Show him the clothes he must change into. I'll take care of his uniform. (*To* ANNA PETROVNA) Attend to this patient, please.

GENERAL: But I'm perfectly fit! There's nothing wrong with me! (*He bends down, picks up a chair by its leg and starts to lift it up. At that moment he collapses unconscious.*)

SERGEYEV: Quickly! Help me!

(*Two* ORDERLIES *enter, pick up the* GENERAL *and carry him into Cubicle No. 8, followed by* ANNA PETROVNA *and* LYUBOV.)

BESSMERTNY: (*Sticking his head out*) Lev Ivanovich, please tell me what's happened. I get the impression it's a very serious accident. There's been nothing about it on the radio.

SERGEYEV: There will be. Bound to be. Keep listening.

BESSMERTNY: I realize you haven't got time for me at the moment. But everyone is inquisitive by nature, and that's why I can't help asking—have they had bigger doses of radiation than me?

SERGEYEV: Much bigger.

BESSMERTNY: In that case you can rely on me. I won't get in your way. Even so, I'd like to be kept in the picture. It's so boring otherwise.

SERGEYEV: (*Grimly*) I guarantee you more than enough entertainment. And there won't be long to wait—just a few hours.

BESSMERTNY: Does that mean some of them have had over a thousand?

SERGEYEV: Even Lydia Stepanovna hasn't been able to measure it exactly. So you must be careful—don't touch any of them. At the same time, I'm counting on your help. Your example is the best treatment they can have—perhaps the *only* one we can give them.

BESSMERTNY: You can rely on me. Remember the good work I did with the fellow who got a dose from the experimental apparatus? He was hoping to live here alongside me, and if it hadn't been for the damage to his esophagus . . . By the way, have you seen the news in the latest issue of the *Journal*? That American, Professor Kyle, reported that bone-marrow transplants can help repair lesions in the alimentary tract too. Apparently the capillaries are restored and so on. The article wasn't very professionally written, but that's the seventh time I've read about this man Kyle. His head's obviously screwed on the right way. He's young too, not yet forty, but he's done a whole series of transplant operations, and all of them have been successful. He's a millionaire, incidentally. And how many operations have you done?

SERGEYEV: About thirty. Unfortunately, by no means all of them were successful. But Kyle really is a good surgeon.

BESSMERTNY: Our Lydia Stepanovna should have been a millionaire long ago! She's got 162 operations to her credit. But she lives in a two-room flat in a high-rise block, Lev Ivanovich. I've told you several times already that we ought to see to it that she's taken better care of.

SERGEYEV: She doesn't bother about such things. She lives alone and she says she doesn't need anything more.

BESSMERTNY: But those tower blocks are cold in winter and hot in summer, Lev Ivanovich. And it should be the other way around. That's why Lydia Stepanovna often spends the night here, and as her boss you find it convenient that she's always on hand for work. But it's not fair, and that's why I think . . .

(VERA *comes out of Cubicle No. 4.*)

SERGEYEV: How is he?

VERA: He's reading. Pulse a little high. Blood pressure almost normal. Slight cardiac arrhythmia. No complaints. I think you may have been mistaken about his dose.

SERGEYEV: I may have been, but not Professor Ptitsyna. She examined your patient.

BESSMERTNY: (*To* VERA) Mild indisposition is the most dangerous condition of all!

VERA: Should I go back to him?

SERGEYEV: You must keep out of the cubicles unless you're specifically needed there.

BESSMERTNY: Don't forget that every one of them is radioactive.

SERGEYEV: Don't frighten her. (*To* VERA) There's no special danger because the background level is low. Even so, you should only go into the cubicles when called for. All information will be shown on the display console.

(ANNA PETROVNA *and two* ORDERLIES *come out of Cubicle No. 8, one of them carrying clothes in a plastic bag.*)

ANNA PETROVNA: He's asleep. Lyuba will stay with him for a little while.

VERA: But there's radiation in there!

ANNA PETROVNA: My dear, there's radiation everywhere here.

SERGEYEV: You can switch on the console.

ANNA PETROVNA: It's working already. I just haven't raised the screen. I'll do it now.

(ANNA PETROVNA *goes over to the Duty Physician's desk and presses a button. A display screen and control console rise upward. Blue, green and yellow lamps indicate the vital data on the patient in each cubicle. No red lamps are glowing; they flash only in case of emergency.*)

(*Looking at the console*) Radioactivity in No. 8 has increased very slightly but still within acceptable limits. (*To* VERA) And remember, no emotion—I asked you . . .

(*Enter* PROFESSOR PTITSYNA.)

PTITSYNA: But why no emotion? Smile, girls. Weep, but smile.

SERGEYEV: At last. Well, what's the situation?

PTITSYNA: About fifty are ours. I've brought the worst ones. And an investigator from the State Prosecutor's office.

ANNA PETROVNA: Why him?

PTITSYNA: He asked to come. He urgently needs to . . .

(*Enter* INVESTIGATOR.)

INVESTIGATOR: It's not much but it's very important. We need statements from everyone who's in a fit condition to write. What happened, where he was, what he was doing. Especially in the first minutes of the accident.

SERGEYEV: I'll see to it.

INVESTIGATOR: In as much detail as possible, please. I can't interview all of them.

SERGEYEV: We'll do it.

INVESTIGATOR: I'll come back tomorrow. I must run now. I have to go to two more clinics.

SERGEYEV: See you tomorrow.

BESSMERTNY: (*Sticks his head out. To* INVESTIGATOR) Do you think it was sabotage?

INVESTIGATOR: Anything's possible. . . . Goodbye.

(*Exit.*)

BESSMERTNY: (*To* PTITSYNA) Greetings, Lydia Stepanovna.

PTITSYNA: Glad to see you in good shape, young man. You must forgive an old woman like me for not having been to see you for three days and then flying away. We've had some trouble, as you can see. Big trouble.

BESSMERTNY: I'm not offended. As soon as you have a moment, look in and see me. I'll be waiting. I want a word with you. Rather a lot of heavy doses, it seems.

PTITSYNA: Big, big trouble. I've never seen anything like it before—and I've been in this business since the very beginning. I was with Kurchatov and Shcholkin . . . with all of them. I can't even believe there could be such a disaster. Ah, here they come. . . .

(*Enter the* CYCLIST, KLAVA, FIREMAN, GEIGER-COUNTER OPERATOR, CONTROL-ROOM OPERATIVE *and* PHYSICIST. *They look around them.*)

CYCLIST: Is this the place? Look—they've put in a row of shower baths. What's the food like here?

PTITSYNA: The food's good. In the meantime, find yourselves an empty cubicle and settle in there.

CYCLIST: It's like a hotel. Better than the Hilton.

SERGEYEV: You can show off your erudition later, but now go in there and get changed.

(*The patients disperse into the vacant cubicles.*)

PTITSYNA: Give them all a tranquillizer. Let them sleep a bit. And girls—be considerate, gentle and kind. They are going to be in pain before too long.

(VERA, NADEZHDA *and* LYUBOV, *together with* ANNA PETROVNA, *go from cubicle to cubicle.* ORDERLIES *carry out plastic bags containing discarded clothes.* PTITSYNA *sinks, exhausted, into an armchair.*)

SERGEYEV: Lydia Stepanovna, please forgive me. At your age you shouldn't have to be flying back and forth, taking on all this work, but instructions came from the top, and they asked especially that you. . . .

PTITSYNA: And quite right too! Any number of local doctors were on the scene, but they lost their heads. Got irradiated themselves. They're keen, but they lacked experience. And, of course, they made a mess of classifying the dosages of radiation. But I'm not surprised. There were some that even confused me: they complain of nausea, dizziness, muscular weakness. Enough to send them straight to the graveyard, but in actuality their doses were trivial. They were simply terrified, so they exaggerated to be on the safe side. But the ones I selected to come here were generally not complaining too much and were behaving calmly. Two of them died at once.

SERGEYEV: I know. One of them from ordinary burns.

PTITSYNA: And radiation burns as well. He died instantly during the explosion.

SERGEYEV: So it *was* an explosion?

PTITSYNA: Of course. It's just that certain people really didn't want it to be an explosion, and they're trying to prove that the reactor failed without blowing up. A fire, they say. Simply a fire.

SERGEYEV: But is there such a big difference?

PTITSYNA: Too big! An explosion is a crime, but a fire is simply professional negligence. And the degree of blame is different. That's why the investigator came here so quickly. However, for them (*Nods towards the cubicles*) it no longer makes any difference *what* it was.

(*Black-out, except for the lights in the cubicles and the glow of burning graphite on the cyclorama.*)

VOICE OF FEMALE RADIO ANNOUNCER: Good evening, listeners. We continue our series of broadcasts entitled *What Everyone Should Know*. The speaker tonight is the Area Chief of Civil Defense, Comrade Nesterov.

MALE VOICE: The explosion of a nuclear bomb is characterized by a blinding flash and a sharp sound like a peal of thunder. After the flash, a fireball forms. The flash is usually visible for more than twenty, even hundreds, of kilometers. At such distances the shock wave may not reach you, but you should nevertheless take protective measures . . . (*The voice gradually fades out.*)

SCENE   TWO

Late the same evening. ANNA PETROVNA *and* VERA *are sitting in the Duty Room.*

ANNA PETROVNA: Well, I don't imagine you expected *this* sort of thing during your attachment here. You were probably looking forward to having a good time in Moscow.

VERA: The people at home envied me. It's hot here, but where I come from there's still snow on the ground. It's inside the Arctic Circle.

ANNA PETROVNA: Did you especially apply to go and work up there?

VERA: My father's in the army. He's been up north for nearly ten years. I've got used to the climate. When we were allotted jobs after medical school, I asked to be sent there.

ANNA PETROVNA: Are you married?

VERA: (*Laughs*) No takers so far. Boys are in no hurry to get married these days. They need a long time to make up their mind.

ANNA PETROVNA: I took the plunge at eighteen. I had Masha when I was nineteen, then my son Andrei came along two years later. Masha's already married, and Andrei's doing his service in the missile troops. No grandchildren as yet, but Masha is abroad at the moment, with her husband in Czechoslovakia, and I suspect they'll bring me a grandson when they come back. Andrei did have a girlfriend, a very nice girl, but he changed his mind or, more likely, they had a row and split up. He never writes about her now.

VERA: (*Nods towards the cubicles*) That boy in No. 3—he's terribly young. Fireman. Probably just out of the army. And now he's here. Is he really going to . . . ?

ANNA PETROVNA: (*Interrupting her*) Don't, Vera, don't think about it.

(*The door of Cubicle No. 6 is opened cautiously; the* GEIGER-COUNTER OPERATOR *creeps out and knocks on the door of No. 7.*)

VERA: Oh, look. I'll go and tell him to get back into his cubicle.

ANNA PETROVNA: No, don't bother. It doesn't really matter. Let him wander about a bit if he wants to.

(*The* GEIGER-COUNTER OPERATOR *knocks again at No. 7. The* CONTROL-ROOM OPERATIVE *opens the door and looks out.*)

CONTROL-ROOM OPERATIVE: What is it?

GEIGER-COUNTER OPERATOR: Aren't you asleep?

CONTROL-ROOM OPERATIVE: Try sleeping here!

GEIGER-COUNTER OPERATOR: Look, it wasn't my fault, it wasn't my fault. . . . You can see for yourself—I've landed up here alongside you. It was so big, the instruments couldn't measure it, don't you see? It was way off the scale!

CONTROL-ROOM OPERATIVE: (*Imitating him, sarcastically*) It was way off the scale! Listen, if me and you had met at a different time and in a different place from this, I'd have knocked you so far off your scale you'd've remembered it for the rest of your life!

(*Slams the door of his cubicle. The* GEIGER-COUNTER OPERATOR *drops wearily into an armchair.*)

ANNA PETROVNA: Your friend seems bad-tempered.

GEIGER-COUNTER OPERATOR: No, he's all right as a rule. When it happened, none of my instruments could measure it because the radiation was so far over the top of the scale. The counter's only calibrated up to a hundred, you see. I thought something had gone wrong. But I just never imagined anything like *this* could happen. . . . He came running up and asked me, "How much?" So I said, "Twenty or so, no more." And he said, "OK," and went over to the reactor. Everything there had gone haywire. He started to mend the cables, so it wouldn't all blow again. He fixed the cables, put in new connectors and, of course, he copped it . . . How the hell was I to know it wasn't twenty but two hundred?

BESSMERTNY: (*Eavesdropping*) Ignorance of the law is no defense. But what was the management doing about it? You must find out. Insist. Get to the bottom of it. Off the scale, indeed. According to Socrates, all our troubles stem from ignorance.

ANNA PETROVNA: You're breaking the rules by leaving your cubicle. That's not like you.

BESSMERTNY: I couldn't sleep. I've been thinking about what happened. Have you heard? They've announced the accident on the radio. Obviously it was something that couldn't be hushed up.

VERA: They're being open about everything now.

BESSMERTNY: Sometimes I think it would be better to keep quiet, so as not to get people worried. When I start thinking about things, for instance, all sorts of rubbish comes into my head. That's why I get all worked up and worried. It's because I know a lot. But he (*Points to the* GEIGER-COUNTER OPERATOR) didn't think, didn't get worried, and he went "off the scale."

(*He returns to his cubicle.*)

GEIGER-COUNTER OPERATOR: But my comrade there has four kids. He's one of the best. Everybody on the station knows him. Got the Order of Lenin last year. He's been there from the word go. He helped to build the station, then stayed on to work there. (*To* ANNA PETROVNA) I didn't know it was two hundred, honestly I didn't. I couldn't even imagine it would be.

ANNA PETROVNA: I believe you.

BESSMERTNY: (*Sticking his head out*) But I don't. You're too kind-hearted, Anna Petrovna. He's killed a famous man and you make excuses for him. Hippocrates said . . .

ANNA PETROVNA: Shut up!

GEIGER-COUNTER OPERATOR: He's right. I've killed a man, as good as . . .

(*The* CYCLIST *comes out of Cubicle No. 1*)

CYCLIST: (*To* ANNA PETROVNA) Look, Mrs. Doctor, fetch us a bottle of vodka, will you? He needs a stiff one, and I need a glass too. He's sniveling like a little kid, and he'll start to howl in a minute. And I've got the shakes, so get us a bottle.

ANNA PETROVNA: There isn't any vodka!

CYCLIST: Don't give me that one! All you doctors keep a bottle of it handy, I know that. Go on, we're meant to have some after all that radiation, for Christ's sake.

(*The* CYCLIST *looks around the hall, goes into the Duty Room and tries to open the drawers of the desk.*)

VERA: Behave yourself!

CYCLIST: Don't you stick your oar in, girl. You're still wet behind the ears, so belt up. I'm very nervous right now. I could easily thump you. Come on, get up! Come here, when I tell you!

VERA: You . . . You . . .

CYCLIST: Well, what *about* me? (*To* ANNA PETROVNA) Come on, let's have the vodka. I'm asking you nicely.

GEIGER-COUNTER OPERATOR: (*Wearily*) Pack it in, for Christ's sake.

CYCLIST: Go on, snivel away then. I'm doing it for your sake, you feeble dolt.

ANNA PETROVNA: All right. (*Goes towards Cubicle No. 1.*) Wait a moment.

(*Exit.*)

CYCLIST: That's more like it. I'll wait. (*Slaps* VERA *on the bottom.*) Not bad. Nice and springy.

VERA: Stop it!

CYCLIST: (*Grinning*) Silly bitch, I just want to give you a little thrill. You'll be thanking me before I'm finished.

(*Enter* ANNA PETROVNA, *holding a bottle of colorless liquid and two medicine glasses. She fills one of them and hands it to the* CYCLIST.)

ANNA PETROVNA: There you are. It's slightly diluted.

CYCLIST: ' (*Sniffing the liquid*) No fooling. Pity you diluted it, though. (*He tosses it back and grunts with pleasure.*) Now that's all right!

ANNA PETROVNA: (*Having poured a glassful for the* GEIGER-COUNTER OPERATOR) Drink it.

GEIGER-COUNTER OPERATOR: I don't want it.

ANNA PETROVNA: It'll steady your nerves. Please.

(*The* GEIGER-COUNTER OPERATOR *drains the glass. The* CYCLIST *starts to yawn.*)

CYCLIST: I feel better already. Nice drop of stuff you've got there, Mrs. Doctor. Let's have another!

ANNA PETROVNA: That'll do till tomorrow.

CYCLIST: (*Yawning, to* VERA) Coming to put me to bed, darling?

ANNA PETROVNA: Go on, off you go.

CYCLIST: Might as well. Feeling pretty tired. Well, good night, all. (*He nods towards the bottle.*) Where d'you keep that stuff? I looked everywhere, couldn't find it.

ANNA PETROVNA: You didn't look hard enough. Off you go.

CYCLIST: I'm ready for a bit of sleep.

(*Exit into cubicle.*)

ANNA PETROVNA: Time for you to go, too. You'll sleep soundly now.

(*The* GEIGER-COUNTER OPERATOR *nods agreement and slowly gets up. Exit into cubicle.*)

VERA: Are they really allowed to have alcohol?

ANNA PETROVNA: It's a sedative. Plus a dash of vodka. You have to play them up sometimes. And aggressiveness is one of the symptoms . . .

BESSMERTNY: (*Sticking his head out of his cubicle*) Sometimes they even go insane. Or they'll be as quiet as lambs and suddenly go berserk. Anna Petrovna has described this phenomenon in detail in her dissertation and has produced some very convincing examples. I remember an American professor described a similar case . . .

ANNA PETROVNA: Look, why don't you try going to sleep? It's going to be a heavy day tomorrow. Would you like some of this too? (*She points to the bottle.*)

BESSMERTNY: No thanks. It has a bad effect on my kidneys. You know it does.

(*He retires into his cubicle and shuts the door. The* FIREMAN *puts his head out of Cubicle No. 3.*)

FIREMAN: Excuse me, may I come out?

ANNA PETROVNA: What for?

FIREMAN: I've written my report on the accident like they asked me to, and I wanted to hand it in.

VERA: How do you feel?

FIREMAN: I've had a good sleep and I feel rested, thanks.

(*The telephone rings in the Duty Room.* ANNA PETROVNA *picks up the receiver.*)

ANNA PETROVNA: No, Lydia Stepanovna, all quiet now . . . We've given them blood and plasma . . . and tomorrow morning . . . No, they're not all asleep, but that's natural—an unfamiliar place . . . so far, normal . . . yes, I'll call you without fail . . . good night.

FIREMAN: (*To* VERA) Can I sit with you for a while? Would you read this through, in case I've done it wrong? (*He hands her several sheets of paper.*)

VERA: I'm afraid I don't know how it's supposed to be done, but anyway . . . (*Reads. She looks up and stares at the* FIREMAN *in amazement.*) So you saw it all?

FIREMAN: First there was a bang, then the blow-out. And right away the roof of the machine room started burning. I set off the alarm signal and climbed up on top myself. It was about thirty meters. The roof was already starting to rock and shudder. I looked at the reactor building and there was a dazzling bright flame. But what was there to burn? Nothing . . . So I suddenly knew—it was the core of the reactor. I was down from that roof in a split second, phoned up the duty officer and told him straight out: "That's no fire, it's an explosion!" Then I got back up on the roof again, and our guys were already there, throwing sand on the burning roof to stop it spreading to the other reactors. . . .

VERA: Weren't you terrified?

FIREMAN: Up there? No . . . later I was, of course. And, well, to be honest, I'm scared now too. Just like it was in Afghanistan.

37

VERA: So you were there too?

FIREMAN: On my military service. I was in the paratroops. It was awful when you were on outpost duty. Especially at dawn, when the mullah starts up that weird sort of noise they make. It was awful because you didn't know anything—the language, the customs, the people. The mountains too. Nothing's like it here. Everything's so different. That's why it's awful.

(ANNA PETROVNA *comes over to them.*)

ANNA PETROVNA: Have you got a girlfriend? I go off duty in the morning, and I could ring her up.

FIREMAN: I haven't got a girlfriend. There's my mother.

ANNA PETROVNA: She can find out everything in the clinic, at the information desk. We'll notify them. Your relatives think you're there. . . .

BESSMERTNY: (*Appearing out of his cubicle*) Hey, fireman, do you play checkers?

FIREMAN: Yes, I do.

ANNA PETROVNA: I warned you. No contact with the patients. And why are you so restless all of a sudden? I've never noticed it in you before.

BESSMERTNY: We've got company now. I want to talk to people. I was getting bored.

FIREMAN: Who's he?

VERA: Bessmertny.

FIREMAN: I don't get it. . . .

ANNA PETROVNA: Our patient. He's been here nearly two years.

BESSMERTNY: This is my four hundred and eighty-eighth day!

FIREMAN: So people *can* survive. . . .

BESSMERTNY: Just two or three games. For mental exercise. By the way, about that crossword clue: "monument" won't fit. The third letter is "R."

FIREMAN: I'm ready.

ANNA PETROVNA: Be careful, now.

BESSMERTNY: He's been processed twice. Back there at the reactor and here in the ultraviolet lobby. So he's even cleaner than I am. All his germs have been killed stone-dead, so he's not dangerous. I've been looking it up in the textbooks. Judging by his distance from the blow-out, he's had the full packet, including neutrons and . . .

ANNA PETROVNA: (*Interrupting*) That's enough. You've gotten too clever for your own good. I have no objection to a few games of checkers.

(BESSMERTNY *goes back into his cubicle.*)

ANNA PETROVNA: (*To* FIREMAN) So you haven't been in love, yet?

FIREMAN: Haven't had a chance to learn.

ANNA PETROVNA: Well, you can start now. Look how pretty our Vera is.

FIREMAN: Right—she is! (*He smiles.*) How do I begin?

ANNA PETROVNA: You've begun already. Just keep it up.

FIREMAN: You're supposed to give a girl flowers, but right now . . .

ANNA PETROVNA: Next time.

VERA: When you two have finished marrying me off . . . !

FIREMAN: Are you married?

VERA: Not yet.

FIREMAN: All right, I might as well begin. You're very sweet and kind and gentle. . . .

ANNA PETROVNA: That's right. You felt it, didn't you, when she was giving you a plasma drip? And a blood transfusion?

FIREMAN: There's not even a bruise where she put the needle in.

(*Enter* BESSMERTNY, *carrying a checker board and box of pieces.*)

BESSMERTNY: If she can do it without bruising you, it's a first-class job. I've been through so many women's hands, I've lost count. You need real talent to do it without bruising. (*To* FIREMAN) I'm used to playing white. You don't mind, do you?

(*They set out the board on a low table. The light in Cubicle No. 7 starts to blink, followed immediately by a flashing red light and a buzzer on the duty physician's display screen.*)

ANNA PETROVNA: (*To* VERA) Come on, Vera—gross arrhythmia.

(*The two doctors rush over to Cubicle No. 7.*)

FIREMAN: What's the matter?

BESSMERTNY: Nothing special. Usual thing—irregular heartbeat. Your move.

FIREMAN: He must be in a bad way.

BESSMERTNY: Who isn't? One, two—and a king. No, that won't work. . . . Oh, come on, play! It's nothing to get worried about. Radiation sickness creeps up on the sly, but when the symptoms are so obvious—like that arrhythmia or nausea—then the doctors can cope with it. They're the best, our doctors.

FIREMAN: Funny . . . I don't feel ill at all.

BESSMERTNY: So thank your lucky stars!

(*The* PHYSICIST *comes out of Cubicle No. 9.*)

PHYSICIST: Would you be very kind and tell me where I could make a phone call?

BESSMERTNY: At the post office, in a phone box or at the railway station.

PHYSICIST: Forgive me, but I know that. I mean, where can I phone here?

BESSMERTNY: I forgive you. Your move, *maestro.* And watch out you don't fall into a trap!

PHYSICIST: Excuse me for distracting you, but I absolutely must make a phone call. I've been doing some calculations. . . .

FIREMAN: You can't phone from here. Don't you realize where you are?

PHYSICIST: Thank you. Of course, I realize where we are, but don't you find such total isolation intolerable?

BESSMERTNY: No, I don't. I advise you to resign, *maestro*.

PHYSICIST: (*Glancing at the board*) Too soon to resign yet. Do you object if I give him some advice?

BESSMERTNY: Yes, I do! If you like, you can put yourself down for a game of "sudden death."

PHYSICIST: Where should I do that?

BESSMERTNY: Join the line, join the line . . . Better still, tell us about these calculations you've been doing.

PHYSICIST: Does it interest you?

BESSMERTNY: We're interested in absolutely everything! After all, the sum total of all mankind's achievements is concentrated within each individual.

PHYSICIST: The whole thing is much simpler than it might seem. The reactor was stopped when it was in an unstable mode, which produced local overheating in one particular sector. Because the emergency system had been switched off, the rise in temperature led to the first, small explosion, which damaged the cooling system. At this point a most peculiar process began to take place: the pressure increased; the water was turned into steam.

FIREMAN: I saw it blowing out. But something like it has happened before.

PHYSICIST: You are absolutely right. But when it happened before, it was brought under control by the fail-safe system. This time, though, it wasn't, and consequently the process accelerated exponentially. Simultaneously with the rapid rise in temperature, practically all the cooling water broke down into oxygen and hydrogen, until finally . . .

BESSMERTNY: The reactor blew itself apart.

PHYSICIST: "Blew itself apart" is absolutely correct—or, to be more precise, it collapsed both towards the machine room and, simultaneously, in the opposite direction. The nature of the reactor's self-destruction is also explicable—or it will be when I've been able to build a mathematical model of it by running it through a computer. That's why I must make some phone calls.

FIREMAN: We've all been asked to write reports. By the way, what do you call them? We call them "reports."

BESSMERTNY: They call it "scientific research." But which stupid bastard—pardon my language—switched off the emergency system?

PHYSICIST: That I couldn't tell you. It was not foreseen in any of the standing instructions.

BESSMERTNY: And do the standing instructions foresee driving through Moscow in the rush hour when your brakes aren't working?

PHYSICIST: I'm sorry, I don't quite follow you.

FIREMAN: What he means is—it's suicide.

BESSMERTNY: No, I didn't mean that at all. I mean it's *murder*. Not suicide—murder! You've won, *maestro*. (*To the* PHYSICIST) Your turn for a game.

PHYSICIST: Thank you, but if you don't mind, I'll go back to my cubicle and do a bit more work on my calculations. If I can't get through and explain them by telephone, I shall have to write them out a bit more fully.

BESSMERTNY: Fair enough. I made the offer, after all. I don't mind admitting that I wanted to get even by beating you.

(*The light in Cubicle No. 7 is now burning steadily, without blinking.* ANNA PETROVNA *comes out of No. 7, followed by* VERA.)

ANNA PETROVNA: One ampule of heart stimulant in two hours' time. We'll prepare him for theater in the morning. (*To* BESSMERTNY) Isn't it time you went to bed? You've had your game, and that's enough.

BESSMERTNY: This is the final game. My revenge on him. Like in the Karpov-Kasparov match.

ANNA PETROVNA: You seem to have turned this place into a games room.

BESSMERTNY: In the West they have exclusive clubs for members only. Full of millionaires, who get together to hatch political plots. Why shouldn't we found a club like that? And give it a suitable name—like The Immortals' Club!

(*The light in Cubicle No. 1 starts to blink, and simultaneously the signal lamps start flashing on the console in the Duty Room.*)

ANNA PETROVNA: (*To* VERA) Quick—antishock procedures . . .

(*They run into No. 1.*)

FIREMAN: Is he having the same trouble?

BESSMERTNY: No, it's a bit more complicated with him. But it's nothing out of the ordinary . . . I think we'd better break it up, you and I. They're not going to let us go on playing anyway. Thanks for a good game. See you tomorrow. (*He starts to go back to his cubicle but stops and turns around.*) Look, fella, you'd better go back inside and lie down. If you really can't stand lying, then get up, but you'd do better to lie down and think of nothing at all. Right now, thinking's

44

not good for you. And when Vera gets some time off, make up to her. Make plans—any sort of plans. Even about marrying her. The bigger and bolder the plans, the better. Don't hold back and don't stint your imagination. If you'd like another game, knock on my door. Don't worry, I've long since gotten used to doing without much sleep. I actually like it when people disturb me—it means I can still be useful.

(*Cubicle No. 4 starts to blink.* ANNA PETROVNA *comes out of No. 1 and strides quickly over to the Duty Physician's desk. Cubicle No. 6 starts blinking.* ANNA PETROVNA *unlocks the telephone cover and dials a number.*)

ANNA PETROVNA: . . . Lev Ivanovich? All hands on deck. It's started! I admit I didn't think it would come so soon. Vera and I can't cope any longer. . . .

(*The light starts to blink in Cubicle No. 5, followed by those in No. 8 and No. 2. As the stage gradually blacks out, the bright-red glow on the cyclorama flares up more and more brightly.*)

MALE VOICE ON RADIO: It is important to know that penetrating radiation can only strike people at a distance not exceeding two or three kilometers from the center of the nuclear explosion. After you have seen the bright flash, the shock wave will reach you a few seconds later. That interval will be enough to take cover in your immediate vicinity or at least to lie down on the ground. . . .

SCENE THREE

Next morning. A brief working conference is in session, attended by SERGEYEV, PTITSYNA, ANNA PETROVNA, VERA *and* LYUBOV. *As usual,* BESSMERTNY *is listening to them from the open door of his cubicle.*

SERGEYEV: Right, that's clear enough. Even so, we will not change the accepted routine. Your report, please, Anna Petrovna.

ANNA PETROVNA: No. 1—condition satisfactory, temperature normal, pulse steady. No. 2—

PTITSYNA: Stop a moment, Anna. Nothing unexpected— that's the main thing. We've coped, Lev Ivanovich. We've coped. And I'm delighted. From now on—as per program. Further transfusions plus intensive therapy.

SERGEYEV: Aren't you tired, Lydia Stepanovna? After all, you've been on your feet nearly all night. Perhaps you'd like to be replaced?

PTITSYNA: By whom? Were you thinking of sending up someone from the botanical department? They only work at the cell level.

SERGEYEV: But, my dear Lydia Stepanovna, why talk like that?

PTITSYNA: I've been telling you for a long time: think of the future. Your staff establishment has been getting bigger, swelling like yeast, yet you cut down the numbers here on the third floor. How many times have I told you—don't forget us. We're slack here only until an emergency comes along. Well, it's come. Are you really proposing to send us botanists? They haven't the nerves for this sort of work. They like a quiet life.

SERGEYEV: But this isn't a full-scale meeting of the Institute staff, Lydia Stepanovna.

PTITSYNA: I'll go for you at the next full meeting too. And you won't get rid of me by pensioning me off either, I'm telling you that straight out. It won't work!

SERGEYEV: The thought has never entered my head. . . .

PTITSYNA: You're a crafty lot, you people in charge of things. You speak nicely to us, then you quietly fix matters among yourselves, behind our backs. Mutter, mutter, rustle, rustle behind the scenes and, lo and behold, a decision has been made, supposedly by "democratic consent." Who took two medical posts away from me last year? I was pacified and told that all was well, that my views would be taken into account and so on and so forth—but you still took my two senior posts and gave them to the gardeners on the first floor. I know whose daughter you were fixing up with a job there. Unfortunately, when I found out, it was too late.

SERGEYEV: Yes, I was guilty. I admit it and I apologize.

PTITSYNA: That's just how you shut me up—you know I love it when people confess. You're a cunning fellow, Lev Ivanovich. But what really saves you is something else. You have golden hands. You would be priceless if you weren't so keen on being a big boss. Your proper place is here, on the third floor. You'd be an academician by now, but you spend your time thinking about how to keep the men in the ministry happy instead of concentrating on science. There are, oh, so many of them, those men from the ministry, and they change so quickly. They come—and they go . . .

SERGEYEV: You seem to be in a rather philosophical mood, Lydia Stepanovna!

PTITSYNA: I'm tired, and that makes me crabby.

ANNA PETROVNA: I'll stay on duty. I'm not too tired.

PTITSYNA: No, I'll manage. You go and rest. And the girls will help me. By the way, there were three of them yesterday. Where's the other one?

LYUBOV: Nadezhda's not here. She left.

SERGEYEV: What d'you mean—she left?

LYUBOV: She packed her things last night. She said, "I can't take it!" and made for the station.

PTITSYNA: Was she afraid of radiation?

LYUBOV: Yes. She said she wanted to have children one day, but the radioactivity here . . .

PTITSYNA: But what about you? Aren't you planning to have children?

LYUBOV: Yes, I am.

PTITSYNA: Then why have you stayed here?

LYUBOV: Somebody has to.

SERGEYEV: I'll deal with this Nadezhda. I have all her papers. I'll write to her bosses.

PTITSYNA: "I'll write . . . !" The girl just lacked guts, that's all. It's a good thing she's gone if she was frightened. Don't spoil her life for her. Fear is like rust. It corrodes very quickly. (*To* VERA *and* LYUBOV) So, my dears, if you're afraid, off you go. We'll manage without you. (*To* SERGEYEV) There's no point in keeping them, still less threatening them, if they don't want to be here. Radiation *is* frightening. It can terrify *anyone*. It used to frighten me— and you, too—but we forgot about it and that's why we're working here.

BESSMERTNY: (*Sticking his head out*) Nadezhda has gone . . . vanished . . . left us. Nadezhda means "hope." How can we survive without hope?

PTITSYNA: Hullo, young man. How did you sleep?

BESSMERTNY: I managed not to have any dreams. Last night they were nightmares—and I was awake.

PTITSYNA: I'm counting on you to keep up our patients' morale. You're our best medicine.

BESSMERTNY: You can rely on me. I've had my first game of checkers.

PTITSYNA: There are still dominoes, chess, crosswords . . . and what else?

BESSMERTNY: Anything you want me to do, Lydia Stepanovna. (*Retires into his cubicle.*)

PTITSYNA: He really is our best form of therapy.

VERA: I'm going to stay here in the Institute. I don't know anyone in Moscow. There's nothing for me to do here. I'll get a few hours' sleep in the rest-room and then come and help you.

PTITSYNA: Thank you.

SERGEYEV: There's one more item for today. The investigator is coming at twelve. (*Sees* PTITSYNA's *perplexed look.*) The point is, that this is the first accident at a reactor. The investigator is in a hurry. First, because eyewitness testimony is essential. And secondly, well, because he doesn't want to be too late before his witnesses. I can't refuse him.

PTITSYNA: But I will only allow him to talk to those who . . .

SERGEYEV: Of course, of course. He understands all that. I must go now. (*Goes towards the door.*) I'll look in at twelve. By then I will have had the answers from the bone-marrow bank. For each patient. Then we must contact the donors.

PTITSYNA: I'll be waiting for you. We're going to have to get a move-on. I'm very worried about No. 4 and No. 7.

SERGEYEV: I'll have information about their donors by noon, then I'll arrange their operations for tomorrow. Will you assist me, or shall I assist you?

PTITSYNA: You go first. I like watching good surgery and I always admire your work. Then I'll do the next batch myself.

LYUBOV: (*Frightened*) The *next* batch?

PTITSYNA: From now on, my dear, we are going to be operating every day. Without any breaks. That's what our job is like.

(*Exit* SERGEYEV. KLAVA, *the peasant woman, comes out of her cubicle.*)

KLAVA: I must go home. My cow, Dasha, hasn't been milked.

LYUBOV: Don't worry. Someone will see to it.

KLAVA: And the chickens haven't been fed.

LYUBOV: Do you live all alone?

KLAVA: Yes, there's only me and Dasha. And she hasn't been milked. Being here's not doing me any good . . .

LYUBOV: It'll be all right. Come along, lie down and rest.

KLAVA: I've got to milk Dasha, or her udder will swell. . . . She'll die.

LYUBOV: (*Trying to lead her back to her cubicle*) I'll call and ask them to milk her. I promise I will.

KLAVA: And tell them to feed the chickens. The grain's in the storeroom at the back. Dasha will get ill. She's all I have.

She's old and ill, but she keeps me in milk. Nearly a bucket-ful a day. Be a dear and ask them. . . . And could they please feed her and water her too? But can they? You see, I've heard tell all the grass will turn to wormwood, and the rivers will run with bitter poison. Oh, dear, I do feel funny. . . .

LYUBOV: Please go and lie down.

(*Exit* KLAVA.)

Lydia Stepanovna, we must call and tell them.

PTITSYNA: There's no point in telephoning.

LYUBOV: Wormwood . . . the rivers running with bitter poison . . . is she delirious?

PTITSYNA: It's like the Apocalypse. It makes people start thinking about God and the Devil.

LYUBOV: How did she land up in here?

PTITSYNA: There was fall-out from the reactor along a six-kilometer-wide strip. She had been digging in her kitchen garden since dawn. And her cow, Dasha, was grazing nearby. So both of them got a massive dose. And the chickens too—although chickens, oddly enough, are very resistant to radiation. No one knows why, but the dangerous dose for them is fifty times higher than for humans. All other living things—people, trees, grass—perish, but chickens are hardly affected. All that happens is that they get aggressive. They'll even attack rabbits. They actually peck through their skulls, like birds of prey.

LYUBOV: How awful.

PTITSYNA: Yes, awful is the word.

LYUBOV: All the same, I'll call about Dasha.

PTITSYNA: There's no point, my dear. Don't tell her, but Dasha and every other living thing in that zone has already been destroyed. It had to be done.

(*The* GENERAL *comes out of his cubicle.*)

GENERAL: Very bad water you have here. I wet my head to comb my hair and my hair's coming out in handfuls. The water's obviously polluted. You must see to it.

PTITSYNA: (*Wearily*) Yes, general.

(ANNA PETROVNA *comes over from the Duty Room.*)

ANNA PETROVNA: (*To* PTITSYNA) I'm going home to rest a bit, then I'll come back. If anything happens, call me.

(*She goes towards the door. The* FIREMAN *comes out of his cubicle, approaches* ANNA PETROVNA *and whispers something to her.*)

I'll do my best. Goodbye for now.

(*Exit.*)

GENERAL: (*To the* FIREMAN) You did a magnificent job. When we get out of here I'm going to recommend you for a decoration. I'm recommending everyone who was in the machine room. And you in particular.

FIREMAN: I was only doing my duty, sir. Thank you.

GENERAL: No need to be so official. We're all off duty now—unfortunately. We don't have to be formal.

FIREMAN: Very good, comrade general.

(*The* DRIVER *comes out of his cubicle.*)

DRIVER: (*Stretching*) I don't think I've ever slept so well in my life.

(The light in Cubicle No. 2 starts to fade. Immediately the red light on the console starts to flash and the buzzer is heard.)

PTITSYNA: *(To* LYUBOV*)* Come on. Cardiac arrest.

(Both go into Cubicle No. 2. The GEIGER-COUNTER OPERATOR *emerges from his cubicle.)*

GENERAL: They have a busy job.

DRIVER: But isn't yours a busy one too, comrade general? If it isn't someone's forgetting to switch off their electric stove, it's spontaneous combustion in a warehouse or a forest fire.

GENERAL: Yes, forest fires—they're a disaster. Do you know how many millions of rubles in loss they cause every year? It adds up to an enormous figure. So you're quite right: there's no tougher or more dangerous job than ours in the fire service. It's like the war—always on active duty.

(The light in Cubicle No. 2 begins to fade. Enter the PHYSICIST.*)*

PHYSICIST: Excuse me, but has the investigator come for our reports?

FIREMAN: Not yet.

PHYSICIST: If I'm not here . . . or if I'm unconscious when he comes, please remind him about my calculations. They're on the bedside table in the cubicle.

FIREMAN: You can give them to him yourself.

*(*BESSMERTNY *appears from his cubicle. He is elegantly dressed for outdoors, complete with bow tie, felt hat, and walking stick. Disregarding everyone, he starts to stroll up and down the stage. For some time they all stare at him in bewilderment.* BESSMERTNY *evidently enjoys the impression he is making.)*

GENERAL: Who is this . . . creature?

DRIVER: The oldest inhabitant. He knows everything about this place.

PHYSICIST: (*To* BESSMERTNY) Excuse me, but do you think we are going to be here for long?

BESSMERTNY: Personally, this is my four hundred and eighty-eighth day here.

DRIVER: But why aren't you . . . wearing one of those overalls?

BESSMERTNY: I do educational work.

GENERAL: With whom?

BESSMERTNY: The whole section. It's a pity that not everybody's here.

(*The* CYCLIST *comes out of his cubicle.*)

CYCLIST: What's happened to the girl with the curly hair? And the older one, the woman doctor?

BESSMERTNY: Dr. Anna Petrovna and Vera, the intern, are now resting after their turn on duty.

CYCLIST: Who's this toffee-nosed bugger?

BESSMERTNY: We must react with calm and restraint to impudence or tactlessness. I shall ignore that remark.

CYCLIST: You won't ignore it if I punch you up the throat.

GENERAL: Don't be rude! Your face seems familiar. Where have we met before?

DRIVER: I know him too. I've seen him somewhere.

CYCLIST: (*Wearily*) You're wrong. I don't come from around here. I don't belong with you lot. (*Retreats into his cubicle.*)

(*The light goes out in Cubicle No. 2.* PTITSYNA *comes out of No. 2, goes wearily over to the Duty Room and starts to write.* BESSMERTNY *follows her.*)

BESSMERTNY: Bad news, Lydia Stepanovna?

PTITSYNA: It's over.

(BESSMERTNY *takes off his hat.* LYUBOV *comes out of Cubicle No. 2. She is crying.*)

GEIGER-COUNTER OPERATOR: (*Shouts*) I don't want to know! (*Rushes into his cubicle and shuts the door.*)

GENERAL: It's all your doing, you physicists. Atomic energy—the future of civilization . . . atomic bombs, reactors, power stations. . . . You dreamed it all up—now look what's happening!

PHYSICIST: Why is it our fault? The reactor is a perfect device. It's a miracle! But you simply can't treat it like . . .

GENERAL: Like what?

PHYSICIST: Forgive me, but you can't treat a reactor . . . carelessly. It can't stand just any sort of handling. It will take a lot, but not everything. Like a human being.

GENERAL: What exactly do you mean?

PHYSICIST: I may be mistaken, of course, but, judging by my calculations, the emergency fail-safe system was switched off. That means there was someone who gave the order to switch it off.

GENERAL: Who?

PHYSICIST: Unfortunately, I don't know.

DRIVER: One of the bosses.

PHYSICIST: You may be right. None of the operatives, for example, would allow himself to take such a decision.

BESSMERTNY: The director of the power station, perhaps?

PHYSICIST: Whoever was in that position could have given the order, but he must have realized what it might lead to.

(*The door of Cubicle No. 5 is flung open and the* DIRECTOR *of the power station strides out.*)

DIRECTOR: I am the director of the nuclear power station. I gave no such order.

(*The stage is gradually blacked out. The light on the cyclorama glows even more brightly.*)

MALE VOICE ON RADIO: Remember that the level of radiation that builds up for an hour after the nuclear explosion will have halved within two hours and in three hours will have reduced to a quarter of its original intensity. Within forty-eight hours the level of radiation and the degree of contamination of foodstuffs will have fallen by a factor of a hundred.

CURTAIN

ACT TWO

The act begins with a repetition of the last few lines of the previous act.

BESSMERTNY: The director of the power station, perhaps?

PHYSICIST: Whoever was in that position could have given the order, but he must have realized what it might lead to.

(*The door of Cubicle No. 5 is flung open and the* DIRECTOR *of the power station strides out.*)

DIRECTOR: I am the director of the nuclear power station. I gave no such order.

PHYSICIST: Excuse me, but someone must have given the order to switch off the emergency system.

DIRECTOR: I can't be responsible for the actions of every lunatic. And leave me alone—I'm ill. Very ill.

BESSMERTNY: Anyone would think all the rest of us were in perfect health.

(*All are silent.*)

DRIVER: The strawberries will be ripe soon.

GENERAL: What strawberries?

DRIVER: The early varieties. Big, sweet ones. Fetch five rubles a kilo.

GENERAL: What have strawberries got to do with anything?

DRIVER: My wife sells them. From our garden. They bring in six or seven hundred rubles a season.

GENERAL: I don't know what you're talking about.

DRIVER: Who's going to buy my strawberries now? Nobody will touch them, even at fifty kopecks a kilo.

BESSMERTNY: You're right there. The "strawberry kings" are ruined. And not just around the power station but in the whole region. They're going to go hungry this year.

DRIVER: Oh, they'll ship their fruit out all right, to the north or to Siberia. But we won't be able to sell ours.

GENERAL: Don't you earn enough?

DRIVER: Can anyone keep a family with two kids on a hundred and thirty a month?

GENERAL: What about bonuses?

DRIVER: They never work out at more than another ten rubles a month.

GENERAL: Why didn't you tell me before?

DRIVER: There was the strawberries, you see. And three apple trees, two plum trees and pears. My pears were big ones. Never had any trouble selling them.

PHYSICIST: I greatly sympathize with your misfortune. But I must point out that strawberries, vegetables, fruit and milk . . .

DRIVER: Klava's cow was there too.

PHYSICIST: You have to be particularly careful about milk. Throughout the whole contaminated zone. Radioactive "dirt" falls, and then the cow eats it along with the grass. No, the contamination of milk is a very serious matter. Calculations show that the danger remains for at least six months.

GENERAL: None of your prognoses, comrade scientist, are worth a bent kopeck.

PHYSICIST: I'm sorry, but I find it hard to agree with that remark.

DIRECTOR: (*Snapping out of his torpor*) He's right. (*Pointing at the* GENERAL) How many times have you told us: "Nuclear power stations are absolutely safe," "Nuclear power stations are totally reliable"? You physicists have done altogether too much talking.

PHYSICIST: Excuse me, but to hear that coming from *you* . . .

DIRECTOR: From me or from anyone else—from him, for example (*Nodding towards the* GENERAL)—what's the difference?

GENERAL: Now, now, it's no good your dragging other people into this! You're the director of the station. You have to take the responsibility.

DIRECTOR: And you don't have to?

GENERAL: Me? I know my duties.

PHYSICIST: Forgive me, but unfortunately there is a great deal that we don't know. A new generation has been born and has grown up at a time when people have been constantly flying around in space and building nuclear power stations. They're thoroughly used to them. And we older ones have failed to get it into our heads that they are dangerous, very dangerous.

DRIVER: The devil's been hiding in them. He was sitting there quietly and waiting. Now he's jumped out. "Here I am," he says!

GENERAL: Superstitious rubbish! I'm surprised at you.

DRIVER: The stronger the head, the weaker the soul.

GENERAL: Pernicious philosophy!

(LYUBOV *comes out of Cubicle No. 6.*)

LYUBOV: (*To* PTITSYNA) He's calmer, but he's not asleep.

PTITSYNA: (*Finishes writing and comes out into the hall. To the* DIRECTOR) Don't worry, I've found out about them.

DIRECTOR: Was it a big dose?

PTITSYNA: Unfortunately, yes, but not lethal. Luckily, they didn't get out of the car. That's right, isn't it?

DIRECTOR: Yes, they were inside all the time. I was the only one to get out.

PTITSYNA: Well, that saved them. In two or three months their condition should be normal.

DIRECTOR: Thanks. Thank you very much indeed.

PTITSYNA: You can thank yourself for not letting them out of the car.

DIRECTOR: What an idiotic business! Idiotic!

(*The* GENERAL *is reading the* FIREMAN'*s report that has been lying on the table.*)

GENERAL: (*To the* FIREMAN) Well done! You behaved splendidly. . . . But there's one inaccuracy here.

FIREMAN: I wrote down just what happened.

GENERAL: What you say about an explosion is incorrect. You didn't pass on that information at the time.

FIREMAN: I told the duty officer in plain language, not in code, that I could see the core of the reactor and that it was open to the air because the top had been blown off. I also told him to pass it on to the proper quarters. I know the standing orders.

GENERAL: What made you decide it was an explosion?

FIREMAN: A black ball, like smoke, was forming over the turbine room and moving upwards.

GENERAL: But over the turbine room and not over the reactor.

DIRECTOR: (*Wearily*) What does it matter? What's the difference?

PHYSICIST: Excuse me, but that piece of information is extremely important.

PTITSYNA: I was at the first Soviet atomic explosion, the very first. I was still young then, terribly young . . . I'm amazed they trusted me enough to send me there because there were plenty more experienced doctors. I was in the bunker along with Kurchatov, Shcholkin, Khariton ... everybody, in fact ... and Beria too. Stalin had put him in charge of developing the bomb. There was one door in the bunker, on the side facing away from the explosion. It was ajar, so that we could see out. Well, when the flash came and then the bang, Khariton rushed to the door to shut it because the shock wave was on its way. But Beria grabbed him, started to hug him and kiss him. Khariton was desperately trying to reach the door and Beria wouldn't let him go.... Everyone was frozen with terror. But he pulled himself free and just managed to close it in time. Oh, God, the nonsense one remembers!

BESSMERTNY: Lydia Stepanovna, that's history.

PTITSYNA: It was long ago—so long ago that I can't quite believe it was me.

PHYSICIST: Kurchatov ... excuse me, but did you really know all those great men?

PTITSYNA: I've even treated some of them. Not always successfully, I'm sorry to say. I must ask you to go back to your cubicles. Lyuba and I will start in a moment. Unfortunately, some of you need another blood transfusion. Not afraid of it, I hope?

GENERAL: If it must be done, it must be done.

FIREMAN: Vera will be back soon. Can I wait for her?

PTITSYNA: There's not always time to wait.

(*The stage is gradually blacked out. As before, the cyclorama glows bright red.*)

MALE VOICE ON RADIO: The threat of a nuclear attack will be announced immediately on the radio, on television and in the press. Wherever you may live, in a town or in the country, when you hear that announcement take immediate protective measures. Remember, in those circumstances, every minute is precious. Above all, secure means of protection for yourself and your family. Prepare a small store of food, water and a home medicine chest, which should include a thermometer, spirit of ammonia, iodine, bandages, cotton-wool, antibiotics and other medication . . .

SCENE TWO

Noon. The light in Cubicle No. 6 is blinking. There is no one in the hall. Enter ANNA PETROVNA. *She goes to Cubicle No. 3 and knocks on the door. The* FIREMAN *looks out.*

ANNA PETROVNA: One red rose, as requested.

FIREMAN: Thank you very much. I promise to settle up with you later.

ANNA PETROVNA: Forget it.

FIREMAN: What about Vera?

ANNA PETROVNA: She's coming soon. She had to go to the telegraph office to tell her parents that she's been held up here.

FIREMAN: But she . . . she will come back, won't she? Perhaps she'll do what Nadezhda did and leave?

ANNA PETROVNA: People either run away from this place at once or never. Women, of course. Men, unfortunately, usually can't stick it out.

FIREMAN: I'll stick it out. Like him. (*Nods towards* BESS-MERTNY's *cubicle.*) I gave you my word, I'll stick it out.

ANNA PETROVNA: I believe you.

BESSMERTNY: (*Puts his head out*) I was starting to miss you, Anna Petrovna. You might as well know—from now on I shall always miss you when you're not here. I'm following the example of the younger generation. If they can fall in love, why can't I?

ANNA PETROVNA: Thanks, my dear. Believe me, I appreciate that very much.

BESSMERTNY: Now we will only say sweet words to each other. Like Tristan and Isolde.

ANNA PETROVNA: I shall obey, my Romeo! But first of all I must examine you and listen to your ticker. We seem to have forgotten you completely in all the rush.

BESSMERTNY: We still have plenty of time before you need do that.

ANNA PETROVNA: Don't argue. Into your cubicle and get undressed.

BESSMERTNY: What, already? I was only just starting to fall in love. I'm only in the first stage. Love comes later. But you want me to strip right away.

ANNA PETROVNA: You're utterly shameless! For prophylactic purposes, and to stop you getting too excited, I'm going to give you a couple of jabs.

BESSMERTNY: Anything you say, my exquisite creature. Only I don't want those jabs that suppress my natural instincts. Let them have full rein!

ANNA PETROVNA: (*Heading for his cubicle*) I'll cool your ardor.

(*Enter* SERGEYEV *and the* INVESTIGATOR.)

SERGEYEV: As far as you can, I beg you to be tactful. They're all at a stage when their reactions are acute. You do understand, I hope?

INVESTIGATOR: I'll ask them only the questions that are absolutely essential.

(*Enter* PTITSYNA.)

PTITSYNA: Their reports are on the table. The man in No. 9 has written a lot.

INVESTIGATOR: I'll just sit down for a while and look through them. Pay no attention to me.

PTITSYNA: The patients in No. 1, No. 5 and No. 8 haven't written anything. And I'm afraid I was too late for the patient in No. 2. . . .

INVESTIGATOR: I'm so sorry. You need say no more.

(*Picks up the sheets of paper and starts reading them. The light in Cubicle No. 3 begins to fade.* PTITSYNA *stares at the console for a long time, sighs and slowly goes over to the* FIREMAN'S *cubicle.*)

SERGEYEV: About the transplants . . . they've found suitable donors for nearly all of them. Except No. 5, the director.

PTITSYNA: Tell me later.

(*She goes into Cubicle No. 3. Enter* LYUBOV.)

INVESTIGATOR: (*To* SERGEYEV) Can I have a talk with the control-room operative?

(SERGEYEV *looks questioningly at* LYUBOV.)

LYUBOV: No. 7? Yes. I'll call him.

(*The* GEIGER-COUNTER OPERATOR *comes out of his cubicle and notices* LYUBOV *going into his neighbor.*)

GEIGER-COUNTER OPERATOR: Will he come out?

LYUBOV: (*Turning back*) He's lying with his face to the wall, not saying anything.

GEIGER-COUNTER OPERATOR: Ask him to come out, dear. I must tell him I didn't know what the radiation level was. I thought it was no more than twenty, but it was two hundred . . .

INVESTIGATOR: Where was it two hundred?

GEIGER-COUNTER OPERATOR: By the transformers. But the level was way off the scale of all my instruments. I thought it was no more than twenty.

INVESTIGATOR: Didn't you have a duplicate set of instruments as a back-up?

GEIGER-COUNTER OPERATOR: Another set of instruments? Where would we get them from? The ones we did have had been repaired over and over again, and anyway they were thirty years old.

INVESTIGATOR: But the station's new. It hasn't been in operation for more than ten years.

GEIGER-COUNTER OPERATOR: What's that got to do with it? Our equipment had been lying in some store somewhere long before the station was even built. They didn't want to write the stuff off, so they sent it to us.

SERGEYEV: That seems hard to believe.

GEIGER-COUNTER OPERATOR: We coped, as long as nothing went wrong. We'd patch it up and go on using it. There was no hurry to get new equipment and we had a good routine going. Inspectors came down often enough from Moscow to check up on us. Everything was always in order. Not one case of over-radiation because they checked that too. No one ever thought the whole thing would blow up.

INVESTIGATOR: Ah, so you think there was an explosion, do you? Did you see it yourself?

GEIGER-COUNTER OPERATOR: People told me. I didn't see it myself.

(*Enter* LYUBOV *and the* CONTROL-ROOM OPERATIVE.)

CONTROL-ROOM OPERATIVE: But I saw it.

GEIGER-COUNTER OPERATOR: I didn't know it was off the scale.

CONTROL-ROOM OPERATIVE: Oh, shut up about your damned instruments! You didn't know what was happening, but I did. I saw the overheated graphite. There were pieces of it on the floor of the reactor hall. Glowing bright blue. (*To* GEIGER-COUNTER OPERATOR) And I didn't need your bloody counters to tell me it wasn't twenty and it wasn't two hundred. It was nearer a thousand!

GEIGER-COUNTER OPERATOR: You saw that, you knew what it was—and you still went in there?

CONTROL-ROOM OPERATIVE: All the fuses on the transformers had blown. And without power you're in trouble because then there's no way of cooling the reactor, so I went in. Told my lads to keep well out of the way . . .

GEIGER-COUNTER OPERATOR: (*To the* INVESTIGATOR) He has apprentices. Boys from the Technical and Trade School. He always had them with him—it's part of their training.

CONTROL-ROOM OPERATIVE: They were kicking up a racket, and I had to shut them up. In the end I sent them home.

INVESTIGATOR: So you knew . . .

CONTROL-ROOM OPERATIVE: Of course I knew. I've been in the nuclear-energy business since the word go. I worked on building the station, then I stayed on at No. 4 Reactor. Lots of us did. It was a good reactor . . . very good.

(*Enter the* PHYSICIST)

PHYSICIST: But someone switched off the emergency safety system!

CONTROL-ROOM OPERATIVE: I don't know about that. Wasn't my business. (*To the* INVESTIGATOR) Mr. Four-Eyes here (*pointing to the* PHYSICIST) was sitting there too, in the reactor hall. I said to him, "Run for it. . . ."

PHYSICIST: Why didn't *you* run for it?

CONTROL-ROOM OPERATIVE: Because my transformers had died on me. I had to get them going.

PHYSICIST: Excuse me, but I couldn't leave either. I was recording the temperatures. I realized that no one besides me was measuring them. The reactor had started to heat up, and it was important to monitor the dynamics of the process. How could I have left?

INVESTIGATOR: You did leave eventually.

PHYSICIST: I'm sorry, but I don't remember that. I was told later that I was carried out unconscious. I'm sorry.

INVESTIGATOR: What about you?

CONTROL-ROOM OPERATIVE: I got away by myself. I switched on the transformers and left. There was nothing more for me to do.

(The light in Cubicle No. 3 goes out, and PTITSYNA, *exhausted, comes out of the cubicle. She looks at them all with an odd expression, but no one pays any attention to her. She goes over to* SERGEYEV *and takes him by the elbow. He understands the situation at once, and they both go into the Duty Room.)*

INVESTIGATOR: *(To the* PHYSICIST*)* I've looked at your calculations but, to be absolutely honest, I can't make sense of them.

PHYSICIST: Give them to the physicists whose names I've put in my report. They'll understand. The chief thing you've got to do is find out who switched off the emergency safety system.

BESSMERTNY: *(Sticking his head out)* Who switched it off? The *system* switched it off. The system which sees to it that nobody takes responsibility.

INVESTIGATOR: We'll get to the bottom of it. . . . *(To the* PHYSICIST*)* I won't keep you any longer.

CONTROL-ROOM OPERATIVE: Can I ask a question? When did they evacuate the town?

INVESTIGATOR: On Sunday morning. Very quickly. It took only two and a half hours. They requisitioned a thousand buses and drove everyone away.

CONTROL-ROOM OPERATIVE: But why didn't they announce it immediately on the local radio? In an hour everyone could have been evacuated on foot.

INVESTIGATOR: They were waiting for a government commission to arrive.

CONTROL-ROOM OPERATIVE: What for? Would the commission have decided any differently? What on earth was the point of waiting?

INVESTIGATOR: Nobody could take the decision.

CONTROL-ROOM OPERATIVE: Could—or would?

INVESTIGATOR: No decision was taken.

CONTROL-ROOM OPERATIVE: Well, you ask them, then: why didn't they take that decision? What's the point of questioning nobodies like us?

INVESTIGATOR: We'll ask them. We most certainly will.

CONTROL-ROOM OPERATIVE: A pity I won't hear the answer . . . I'll go back to my cubby-hole if I'm not needed any more. (*To* GEIGER-COUNTER OPERATOR) And you tell the investigator how many times you asked them to give you new instruments.

GEIGER-COUNTER OPERATOR: Four times.

CONTROL-ROOM OPERATIVE: And we bust our guts to speed things up, make promises. "Yes, we'll finish it three months ahead of schedule," "We'll have it working forty-eight hours ahead of time." But when he asks for a proper set of Geiger counters, nobody up top lifts a bloody finger. Yet we always do what the bosses ask *us* to do. . . . Now, why is it like that? We ask *them*—not a dicky-bird. But when they ask *us*, it's "Come on, lads!" and off we go.

INVESTIGATOR: When you said "three months ahead of schedule," were you referring to starting up the reactor?

GEIGER-COUNTER OPERATOR: Yes, that's right. Now that they've got to deal with the accident damage, they'll never find out what went wrong with the reactor. The construction boys were chased out of that foundation pit as if they were jet-propeled, so that the reactor could be handed over

ahead of schedule. Under that reactor there's not only concrete blocks: if you were to poke around down there, you'd
find a couple of excavators too. And all because of the
bonuses they'd get if it was done before the original delivery
date. What good was all that hurry? It's the same as if you
let all the cars belt around town at a hundred kilometers per
hour just for the sake of speed. Doesn't matter if they run
everyone over, just so long as they go faster . . .

INVESTIGATOR: And when you said "forty-eight hours," was
that the reactor?

CONTROL-ROOM OPERATIVE: They promised to have it working on full power right after the holidays. Two days ahead
of schedule. They take on obligations like that all the time.
And how can we refuse to go along with them?

PHYSICIST: And that's why the emergency safety system was
switched off?

CONTROL-ROOM OPERATIVE: I don't know anything about that,
so I can't say. But I really felt pissed off about No. 4 Reactor.
It was a good machine. Better than the others. Yet it had to
happen to that one. . . . When there's an accident in a
chemical factory, hundreds of people die. Planes crash—the
same thing. And what about earthquakes? Whole cities in
ruins. Even space ships blow up at the launch. And all this
in what's supposed to be the age of chemistry, atomic power
and space travel . . .

BESSMERTNY: (*Sticking his head out*) It's not the age of the
atom—it's the age of disaster!

CONTROL-ROOM OPERATIVE: It's a pity, but everyone's going
to think that now. A pity, because our reactors are the
best. . . . Well, I'm going. I don't feel too good.

INVESTIGATOR: Thank you. We'll sort this business out and find out who's to blame.

CONTROL-ROOM OPERATIVE: I hope to God you do. Then there will have been some point in not running away. But if you don't, we've given it all up for nothing.

(*Exit.*)

PHYSICIST: Excuse me, but I must second the comrade's opinion. The chief thing about this tragedy is the lessons we must learn from it. We haven't the right *not* to draw the proper conclusions. It would simply be irrational if we didn't. The experimental data available to us are enormous—in all areas.

(*The* GENERAL *comes out of his cubicle and listens to the conversation.*)

INVESTIGATOR: Experimental data?

PHYSICIST: I'm sorry, perhaps I didn't express myself clearly enough. You see, there has been no such experiment as this in the whole history of science—the explosion of a reactor and its consequences. It may even be the *only* instance of its kind—or rather the first. We must, however, see to it that it's the last. And for that we must study it from every aspect—theoretical, technical, psychological. Absolutely comprehensive study. Not formal and superficial, but profound and from all angles.

INVESTIGATOR: What about Hiroshima and Nagasaki? After all, that was something similar.

PHYSICIST: I'm sorry, but they cannot be compared with Chernobyl. In Japan, everything was destroyed. Instantly. From the shock wave and from radiation pressure. And the Americans haven't yet published all their data on radiobiology. They immediately declared their work in that area to be classified information. Here, after Chernobyl, the situation is different. Here they're saying, the atomic devil has jumped out at us. Well, believe it or not, they're right. Before, we physicists seemed to know all about the devil, but I'm sorry—we didn't. So we must study him. Believe me, the value of this experience is priceless. I know that sounds cruel and callous, but it is priceless.

INVESTIGATOR: One more question. As far as I know, you're not a member of the power station staff, are you?

PHYSICIST: No, I'm from Moscow, from the Institute of Applied Atomic Energy Research. I'd been sent to the station on an assignment. While the reactor was shut down for maintenance, all the instrumentation had to be checked and recalibrated.

INVESTIGATOR: And you stayed there after the explosion?

PHYSICIST: I'm sorry to have to repeat myself, but it was essential to know the specifics of the rise in temperature. Afterward, you see, the reactor would start to cool down in practically the same pattern. Apart from me, there was no one to do that. How could I leave?

GENERAL: The others all left. I saw them.

INVESTIGATOR: They ran—headlong.

PHYSICIST: No doubt they were no longer needed there. That's all.

(PTITSYNA *comes over to the* PHYSICIST.)

PTITSYNA: I'm taking him now.

INVESTIGATOR: Thank you. And good luck!

PHYSICIST: You must pass on my calculations. They are important.

INVESTIGATOR: It'll be done today.

PHYSICIST: Thank you very much. (*To* PTITSYNA) Have you decided?

PTITSYNA: Lev Ivanovich, Lyuba and I are going to do a few of our magic tricks on you. We've found a splendid donor, a gorgeous country girl.

PHYSICIST: Thank you. And one more thing: don't tell my wife and son anything about me yet. They're both physicists, so they will immediately understand. My wife works in the same research institute as myself. Our son's in a nuclear submarine. They don't yet know that I was there.

PTITSYNA: But . . .

PHYSICIST: Let them find out later. About everything that happened. And about my calculations. They'll be proud of me . . . I was the first person in the history of science to do them. It will soften the blow for them. . . .

PTITSYNA: I think you're mistaken. . . .

PHYSICIST: Forgive me, but I must insist on your carrying out my request.

(PTITSYNA *and the* PHYSICIST *go into Cubicle No. 9.*)

GENERAL: People keep talking about an explosion, but frankly I doubt whether there was one. A serious fire—that's another matter. . . .

INVESTIGATOR: But it was one of your own firemen who wrote in his report: "The roof had been blown off the reactor and I looked down into it."

GENERAL: Overexcitement. One always has to make an adjustment for statements made under stressful conditions. . . .

INVESTIGATOR: And is that the reason why you didn't report an explosion?

GENERAL: What do you mean by that?

INVESTIGATOR: Your first report to the Council of Ministers of the Ukrainian Republic. And your second report too.

GENERAL: I must explain . . .

INVESTIGATOR: That's exactly what I want you to do.

(*The door is flung open. Two* ORDERLIES *bring the* CYCLIST, *his arms twisted behind his back.*)

ORDERLY: We're bringing him back. He was trying to run away.

CYCLIST: Let go of my arms, you bastards!

(*The* DRIVER *looks out of his cubicle.*)

GENERAL: (*To* DRIVER) Come here. We'll give our evidence together. (*To* INVESTIGATOR) He was alongside me all the time. He'll corroborate whatever I may say.

INVESTIGATOR: I believe you anyway. (*To* CYCLIST) Why did you try to run away?

CYCLIST: If you like it here, then stay here. I prefer to be out there (*Points to door*), but the guards here are even quicker off the mark than the ones in the clink. They've got electronic alarms. Press a button and they start ringing all over the place.

(*Enter* ANNA PETROVNA, *who goes up to the* CYCLIST *and feels his pulse.*)

CYCLIST: Normal. I only got down to the first floor. If it hadn't been for that bell . . . Can you give me some more of that drug? It's muck, but if there's nothing else . . .

ANNA PETROVNA: Not now. I'll give you some this evening. (*To* ORDERLIES) Let him go now. He won't run away again.

(*Exeunt* ORDERLIES *and* ANNA PETROVNA.)

CYCLIST: We'll see about that. . . .

INVESTIGATOR: (*To* GENERAL) Let's continue. First. Your signature is on the certificate of acceptance of No. 4 Reactor when it was completed and handed over.

GENERAL: Not only No. 4. All of them. I've been working here for fifteen years.

INVESTIGATOR: Yes. And on the certificate of acceptance of the turbine room too?

(*The* DIRECTOR *of the power station comes out of his cubicle, sits down beside the* GENERAL *and follows the conversation attentively.*)

GENERAL: Naturally.

INVESTIGATOR: And no one forced you to sign the certificates?

GENERAL: That's a pointless question. Since I signed them, that means I agreed to the acceptance.

INVESTIGATOR: Are you familiar with the details of the fire at the textile factory in Bokhara twelve years ago?

GENERAL: It's a classic case. . . .

INVESTIGATOR: Yes or no?

GENERAL: Of course I'm familiar with it.

INVESTIGATOR: And the factory on the Baikal–Amur railway line? Both at Bokhara and on the Baikal–Amur line the factory roof was made of highly inflammable materials. Both places burned to a cinder in five or six minutes. The persons responsible were tried and convicted.

GENERAL: Yes, but . . .

INVESTIGATOR: Then why did you sign the certificate of acceptance for the turbine room, when the roof was made of that same material and you knew very well that its use in industrial buildings had been forbidden?

GENERAL: I raised an objection. I informed senior officials at the ministry.

INVESTIGATOR: Yet you signed the certificate all the same.

GENERAL: But you know that the power station was accepted from the builders at the very highest level. My signature was a pure formality. (*Points at the* DIRECTOR) He signed too, you know. We all did. It's just a piece of paper. A formality, that's all.

INVESTIGATOR: But the fire in the turbine room wasn't a formality. It went up like gunpowder. The roof melted, the stanchions were collapsing and the firemen risked their lives to put out that fire on a roof made of material that was banned for such use twelve years ago. (*To* DIRECTOR) Why was that material used here?

DIRECTOR: There was a lot of it in stock. There was a hitch in the supply of other materials, in spite of which the builders handed over the station three months ahead of schedule.

INVESTIGATOR: I see. . . .

GENERAL: What do you see? What did our signatures mean? If I hadn't signed, somebody else would have. When were you born—yesterday? Or do you only ever sign anything when your conscience it totally clear?

INVESTIGATOR: All right, we'll leave that point for the moment. Now, I understand you reached the site an hour after the alarm had been given.

GENERAL: To be precise, forty-six minutes after receiving the information.

INVESTIGATOR: Why?

GENERAL: What d'you mean, why? To assess the situation on the spot. To work out the strategy and tactics for extinguishing the fire. To ensure . . .

INVESTIGATOR: (*Interrupting*) You were informed, were you not, that it wasn't only a fire but an explosion?

GENERAL: I found it hard to believe at first. Anyway, who could have imagined that happening?

DIRECTOR: That's right. Nobody could. . . .

INVESTIGATOR: Did you pass on the information about an explosion to the proper quarters? Yes or no?

GENERAL: I telephoned the Council of Ministers of the republic. I was told: "Don't be an alarmist. Get on with your job—and your job is to put out fires. Make sure the fire is put out as quickly as possible." And I did.

INVESTIGATOR: And three hours later you reported that the fire was extinguished, is that right?

GENERAL: Yes, I did. . . . By the way, what right have you to interrogate me? You'd better talk to the people I reported to. And I did report! I did!

INVESTIGATOR: You drove in your car right up to the reactor building. Did you or did you not know that in terms of radiation safety that was absolutely not permissible?

(*The* GENERAL *does not reply.*)

Did you know or didn't you?

DRIVER: The comrade general told me it was safe there. If the reactor had collapsed inwards, then all the radiation was inside and couldn't get out through the concrete walls. That's what he said.

INVESTIGATOR: Let's talk about something else. Why didn't the firemen have any protective clothing? Not one of them did. According to the regulations, everyone in the fire-fighting unit of a power station must be supplied with protective clothing.

(*The* GENERAL *does not reply.*)

DIRECTOR: It was considered to be unlikely—or, rather, totally impossible—that it would ever be needed.

INVESTIGATOR: In other words, you economized on the firemen's protective clothing?

GENERAL: I will not answer! I will not! You have no right to interrogate me!

(*The* CYCLIST *comes over to the* INVESTIGATOR.)

CYCLIST: I'm the one they call "the Cyclist."

INVESTIGATOR: Well, what of it?

DRIVER: I remember! The police are after him. He's a dangerous criminal—robbery with violence. Always goes about on a bicycle.

CYCLIST: Right, that's me. When I was a lad I was a racing cyclist. Almost got the title of "Master of Sport," then I broke my leg. Smashed up my whole life with it. Three convictions. I've done time, and now I'm on the run. I'm "the Cyclist"! I was doing a couple of jobs in the town near the power station. The pickings were thin—three hundred rubles and a pair of earrings. I was riding my bike over the bridge when that thing, the atom thing, blew up. They caught me on the far side of the bridge, stripped me to the buff and burned the lot, so there's no evidence. . . .

INVESTIGATOR: Why are you telling me this? Is this a voluntary confession?

CYCLIST: Look, Mr. Investigator, you can arrest me now, but the few bits I pinched from those houses are chickenfeed compared with what *he's* done. (*Points to the* GENERAL.) You can get me for breaking and entering—but what are you going to get *him* for?

GENERAL: Be quiet, you criminal!

(*He turns sharply around and goes into his cubicle.*)

CYCLIST: (*To* INVESTIGATOR) Go on, take me. (*Holds out his arms.*) Or didn't you bring any handcuffs with you? I knew what I was doing by coming to you. Just thought I'd give you a bit of a fright. . . .

(*The* CYCLIST *slowly collapses, unconscious.* ANNA PETROVNA *catches him as he falls.*)

ANNA PETROVNA: Help me.

(*Helped by the* INVESTIGATOR *and the* DRIVER, *she carries the* CYCLIST *into his cubicle. The* INVESTIGATOR *and the* DRIVER *return to their places.*)

INVESTIGATOR: (*Wiping sweat from his forehead*) Phew, that was a nasty moment.

DRIVER: You shouldn't have gone for the comrade general like that. He's all right. Always helps me if I ask him. Got my little girl into a hospital. I don't suppose it was his fault. He just did his job like everybody else.

INVESTIGATOR: But he has . . . (*Searches for the right words.*) . . . put your life in danger. Yet you . . .

DRIVER: I think the comrade general feels very bad about all this. About . . . well, about not knowing the radiation was so dangerous. After all, I didn't know either. I've never done any studying about it. Maybe I should've read some books about radiation, but I prefer spy stories and detective stories. The comrade general, he prefers books about love. It seems he shouldn't have been reading about love but about radiation. But does anyone know when a brick's going to fall on his head? And he got a big dose of that radiation himself.

INVESTIGATOR: We're too kind-hearted. Pity.

DIRECTOR: Is kindness a bad thing?

INVESTIGATOR: It depends on the kindness—who, what, when . . .

(*Enter* VERA. *She looks around, then cautiously opens the door of Cubicle No. 3 and slips inside.*)

DIRECTOR: My turn to be questioned, it seems. Well, ask away!

INVESTIGATOR: I have only a few questions. You and I already have a pretty clear picture of things, I think. You were not at the power station all the time, were you?

DIRECTOR: I wasn't able to be, but I was at the very beginning.

INVESTIGATOR: Did you realize at once what had happened?

DIRECTOR: More or less. In general terms.

INVESTIGATOR: And you left the station?

DIRECTOR: I, er, temporarily absented myself. You see . . .

INVESTIGATOR: I know. Your grandchildren were alone at home.

DIRECTOR: I saw that work was in hand to extinguish the reactor. My son's mother-in-law lives in a village nearby, eight kilometers away. I thought I'd just dash over to the village, leave my grandsons there and come straight back.

INVESTIGATOR: But why didn't you alert the whole town? Then they could all have dashed out into the country, even if only, say, five kilometers up-wind. They could have gone that far on foot. It only needed an announcement on the local radio to notify everybody. There was no need for them to wait those twenty-four hours until the official evacuation order was given.

DIRECTOR: It's not as simple as that.

INVESTIGATOR: But to put your grandsons into your car and drive away—that was simpler, was it? After all, you knew better than anyone else what had happened. Yet children were still playing football in town *this morning*. And freshly picked cucumbers were being brought in and sold on the streets. . . .

DIRECTOR: I couldn't get back. You know why. They must have told you.

INVESTIGATOR: Yes—a silly accident. Your car skidded off the road and got stuck on the verge for a quarter of an hour. Fortunately, your grandsons didn't get out of the car. Yes, I know about that. And on the way back you were stopped and detained for a medical check.

DIRECTOR: I had driven right through the "dirtiest" area of the fall-out.

INVESTIGATOR: I want to ask you about something else. I've been looking through your personal file. School, university and so on. By the way, it seems you weren't exactly an outstanding pupil at the Institute of Applied Physics—just average. Even so, you were the only graduate in your year to get a job running a nuclear power station. None of the others made it. How do you explain that?

DIRECTOR: I know I wasn't a high flyer. But I worked hard— and presumably better than the others—and that was why I got the promotion. Don't worry, nobody pulled strings for me. My father's not a minister. My father-in-law is an ordinary worker. Nobody gave me a helping hand. I did it all myself.

INVESTIGATOR: You did it all yourself. I see. . . . And do you know why your predecessor in the job was sacked?

DIRECTOR: Everybody knows why. He was a troublemaker. Plus four reprimands for failing to reach his output targets.

INVESTIGATOR: Yet at the station everybody speaks of him with respect. Even with fondness, one might say.

DIRECTOR: All I know is that the authorities found him difficult to get on with.

INVESTIGATOR: Of course. Because he didn't always do as he was told. He used to argue decisions, in fact. Incidentally, on the question of putting No. 4 Reactor on-line ahead of schedule—he was dead against it.

DIRECTOR: That was a matter for decision by higher authority. They're not stupid, the people in the ministry. They know the overall situation and the state of affairs at our station too.

INVESTIGATOR: Why did *you* never raise any objections? Or was there no cause to do so?

DIRECTOR: Why do you put it like that—"raise objections"? I wrote to them. I made requests. In other words, I did my job in the way it's supposed to be done.

INVESTIGATOR: And without getting any reprimands?

DIRECTOR: Yes, without a single reprimand. Is that bad?

INVESTIGATOR: Your predecessor had four reprimands and not a single accident. You got no reprimands but you've had a major disaster.

DIRECTOR: I knew that was coming. In other words, you're looking for a scapegoat, aren't you? Well, it won't work.

INVESTIGATOR: You're right, you're hard to pin down. You've managed to wriggle away fairly successfully so far.

DIRECTOR: I tell you, you're wasting your time trying to pin the blame on me. I've been asking myself the question: why did this happen? And I can't find the answer. Pure chance, that's all. Go and see other nuclear power stations—take a good look. Were we any worse than them? No, and I can tell you this with authority because I've seen many of them.

We were better. We've won the ministry's efficiency award three times, and our output has always been up to target. So don't come *here* looking for the culprits. *We're* not the ones to blame. But can you explain to me why the quality of nuclear power-station equipment has gotten steadily worse over the past ten years? Why we are given obsolete instruments and spare parts? And, finally, why our requests for the repair of those very same faulty switches, for instance, take three months to reach the ministry and the replies take three months to come back? I could give you dozens more "whys" of that sort—and I'm not the only one. Ask the hydroelectric boys and the people who run coal-fired stations; they have exactly the same problems. And it's no better on the mechanical engineering side or in electronics either. It just so happened that the boil burst at *our* nuclear station. It had to come, but it was still just an accident. Now, you're in the Prosecutor's office. Have you heard what happens when managers of the big Moscow stores are given their jobs? You haven't? Well, I'll tell you. When a manager is selected and confirmed, they say to him: "We know you'll be on the fiddle, and we won't touch you, but don't take it amiss if we put you in jail one of these days—it's all part of the system. Every year we have to take one store manager to court and make an example of him to pacify public opinion. So keep on fiddling till it's your turn to be this year's scapegoat . . ." And, of course, he does just that, so that his family will be provided for while he's doing his stint behind bars and, when he comes out, he'll still have enough put away for the rest of his days.

INVESTIGATOR: If that's your philosophy of life, how did you manage to run a nuclear power station?

DIRECTOR: Were there ever any complaints about me until

this happened? No, there weren't. The reports and comments were never anything but excellent. You can check. It's all on record.

INVESTIGATOR: Nevertheless, the director of another nuclear plant, the one nearest to yours, raised the alarm as soon as the radiation level started rising. He thought something had happened at *his* station.

DIRECTOR: That just goes to confirm what I was saying. He thought it had happened at *his* station. But I didn't think it *could* happen at mine—that's the difference. By the way, I don't think it will come to the crunch in my case.

INVESTIGATOR: So I wish you a successful recovery. . . .

DIRECTOR: No, I don't mean that. (*Points to the cubicles.*) If I get out of here, you and I won't be meeting again. They'll give me the sack, of course—but put me on trial? No, no. In an affair like this they'd have to try too many others as well. It would start a chain reaction that might become unstoppable. You know, it would be much better to forget about this accident altogether . . . better for everyone. And that's what'll happen, I'm telling you, because it's bad news for plenty of others besides myself—others who are much, much higher up the ladder than me. Life was nice and peaceful—and suddenly a reactor blows up! Almost as if it was done on purpose. . . . Like sabotage, you might say.

BESSMERTNY: (*Sticking his head out of his cubicle*) No, it's too easy to blame all your mistakes on the beastly imperialists!

INVESTIGATOR: Are you feeling unwell?

BESSMERTNY: You're building the pyramids—the tombs of the pharaohs. You're our nuclear pharaoh!

DIRECTOR: (*To the* INVESTIGATOR) He's gone right off his head.

BESSMERTNY: Me? What makes you think so? I'm just taking a very sober, realistic look into the future, tens of thousands of years ahead—I am immortal, after all! Just imagine: none of us will be here, not even our great-great-grandchildren. All our cities will have gone. . . . Even the pyramids of Egypt will be just a handful of dust, yet the sarcophagus around this reactor of yours will still be standing. The pyramids of the pharaohs have been there for a mere five thousand years. But to contain the radiation your nuclear pyramid must remain for at least a hundred thousand years. (*Bitterly*) That's some monument to leave our descendants, isn't it?

DIRECTOR: (*To* INVESTIGATOR) He's the one (*Nodding towards* BESSMERTNY) you want to talk to. He knows everything. Well, goodbye. I have the right not to answer your questions. Wait till I get out of here . . .

(*The* DIRECTOR *retires into his cubicle.*)

BESSMERTNY: (*To* INVESTIGATOR) I have just one question to put to you. Are you *really* intending to bring him (*Points towards the* DIRECTOR'*s cubicle*) and the rest of them to court and try them? Or are you just doing all this to give them a fright?

INVESTIGATOR: In my opinion, there must be a trial. And an open trial, what's more.

BESSMERTNY: Do you think you'll manage it?

INVESTIGATOR: I don't know, but I'm going to try.

BESSMERTNY: Have you always succeeded in doing what you wanted to do?

INVESTIGATOR: Not always, but often.

BESSMERTNY: In that case you have my blessing.

INVESTIGATOR: (*Smiling*) Thank you. But not everything is within our power.

BESSMERTNY: It can be, if you want it badly enough.

INVESTIGATOR: Your doctors seem to have been held up.

BESSMERTNY: They're doing an operation. It's hard to say when they'll be finished. You must come here more often. There's still a lot to be cleared up.

INVESTIGATOR: I have two more calls to make at another hospital. There are a large number of witnesses there. I must ask them a few questions.

BESSMERTNY: To rise again from the ashes, one must go through all the circles of hell. Only then can one enter purgatory.

(*Exit* INVESTIGATOR. ANNA PETROVNA *and* VERA *come out of Cubicle No. 3.* VERA *is crying.*)

ANNA PETROVNA: Don't, my dear. Tears won't help any more.

VERA: (*Sobbing*) The rose was lying on his chest. He was carefully holding it to his body.

ANNA PETROVNA: It was for you. He meant to give it to you.

VERA: I ran down to the telegraph office and booked a long-distance call. I wanted to speak to his mother, but there was no reply. I was going to say that his condition was normal and he was doing well.

ANNA PETROVNA: It's a good thing you didn't get through.

VERA: Please, Anna Petrovna, could I go in and be with him

for a little longer? Take another look at him? His face was so peaceful, as if . . .

ANNA PETROVNA: Too late now. No one will see his face again. A lead coffin and a concrete sarcophagus . . . It has to be like that because his body is emitting two or three roentgens an hour. And it will go on doing so for several decades. I'm afraid you can't go in there again.

(*The light in Cubicle No. 8 starts to blink.*)

Quickly! And wipe away your tears. You must always go into a cubicle with a smile. They're waiting for your smile. Come on, girl.

(*Lights are blinking in Cubicles No. 8, No. 6 and No. 4. The glowing of burning graphite still shines brightly on the cyclorama.*)

MALE VOICE ON RADIO: The decision to start evacuation and the details of how it is to be done will be announced on radio and television, published in the press and brought by suitable means to your workplace or homes. The civil defense authorities will undertake to organize food for the evacuees, but if you have a small store of foodstuffs at home, you should take them with you. Remember—in case of a nuclear attack, you must show the maximum caution and self-discipline . . .

SCENE THREE

The afternoon of the same day. There is no light in Cubicle No. 9. SERGEYEV, PTITSYNA, ANNA PETROVNA, VERA *and* LYUBOV *are sitting in the armchairs center-stage.* BESSMERTNY, *as usual, is listening to their conversation.*

SERGEYEV: All of them are in a state of depression.

PTITSYNA: The time has come. They'll all be feeling pain. (*To* LYUBOV) Have you given them painkillers?

LYUBOV: Yes.

VERA: They're not talking. Not a word.

SERGEYEV: Symptom of depression . . . Do you remember our first one, Lydia Stepanovna? I feel a sense of doom, as I did then.

PTITSYNA: Pull yourself together. We haven't the right to give way to such feelings. This first patient of ours couldn't have survived anyway, and you know that perfectly well. Now, though, we might have saved him, so these two decades haven't passed in vain.

SERGEYEV: I had no idea that the physicist got such a massive dose.

PTITSYNA: He was alongside the reactor. And he knew he wouldn't survive—that's why he was in such a hurry to finish his calculations. And he finished them. He'll have a permanent place in the history of science.

SERGEYEV: The price he paid was too high.

PTITSYNA: Who knows the true price of our life? How do you measure it? By what price list?

VERA: Is that really . . . all there is? So what is all this for? (*Points around her at the cubicles*)

PTITSYNA: It's so that others will survive, my dear. Others . . . but, unfortunately, in the future . . .

SERGEYEV: I can't get used to the idea. I'll never learn to.

PTITSYNA: Thank God for that. As soon as you start getting used to it, it's time to go. Retire at once.

VERA: Do none of them have a chance?

ANNA PETROVNA: Of course, some of them have. (*Points towards* BESSMERTNY's *cubicle.*) He didn't seem to have a chance, but he's still alive.

SERGEYEV: I think there's been an improvement in No. 5's liver and lungs. But he needs a bone-marrow transplant. He needs it more than the rest, but there's no donor. There are donors for all the others, but for the one who could really be helped by a transplant there isn't. It's so frustrating. . . .

PTITSYNA: What about that American professor who's flown in? He said at the press conference that he could immediately apply to the American and European banks for donors. Perhaps there'll be one there.

SERGEYEV: They'll apply, but it takes so long. They have to find a donor, then bring him here. . . . It takes so *long!* I sometimes despair at our own helplessness.

LYUBOV: From now on I'm going to be dreaming about this every night.

PTITSYNA: Do you think I don't dream about it? I've been having nightmares for the best part of forty years. Nonstop.

LYUBOV: But that can make you crazy.

PTITSYNA: People have gone out of their minds in this job. But what can you do? There's no one else, only us. Who but us would do a job like this?

LYUBOV: I'm going to leave. . . .

PTITSYNA: I won't try to hold you back. But I don't believe you two girls will go. I think you'll apply to come here for good. And he (*Nodding towards* SERGEYEV) will accept you. He will have to accept you because you won't be able to work anywhere else, only here. There was a time when Anna and I were like you. One day we stayed here, and we found we couldn't go away. Because out there, in the street, life is different. Fresh, I suppose . . . but here, girls, there is pain, unstoppable pain. Each of them (*Nods towards the cubicles*) is suffering, and that pain is our life. When Anna and I have gone, you will stay here. And later other girls like you will come, and you'll teach them how to carry the burden of that pain in their hearts. And you will find that you will always have a pain *here*. . . .

(*The telephone rings.* ANNA PETROVNA *picks up the receiver, then nods at* SERGEYEV.)

ANNA PETROVNA: It's for you, Lev Ivanovich. From the ministry.

SERGEYEV: (*Into the receiver*) Yes, speaking . . . must he? Things are pretty bad here. There's nothing to boast about. . . . Well, you know best, I suppose . . . if you insist . . . I'll be here to meet him. . . . (*Replaces receiver.*) Talk of the devil. That was Kyle. He's coming to see us. He wants to see for himself how things are.

PTITSYNA: Where else could he see anything like it?

SERGEYEV: They'll be arriving in a few minutes. Tidy the place up. This is the first time an American professor has been here. So be on your toes. He's coming to us as a consultant.

PTITSYNA: We'll see what advice he has to offer us.

SERGEYEV: Now, Lydia Stepanovna, be civil to him, please. This has high-level political implications. He'll be talking to the press and telling them what he saw. Over there in the West, they believe what he says.

PTITSYNA: Pity they don't believe *us* . . . Don't worry, Director, we'll give him VIP treatment.

(*Exit* SERGEYEV.)

VERA: (*Pointing at the cubicles*) I'll go and see how they are.

PTITSYNA: Off you go, girls! I'm going to have a little rest. I feel a bit tired. And I don't need to put on any make-up: an old woman's an old woman.

LYUBOV: Oh, come on, Lydia Stepanovna. . . .

PTITSYNA: Go on, my dear. I was just boasting. Do you think I don't want to show off in front of an American? I'll be ready when they're finished putting on their overalls and going through the procedures. I'll be ready.

(ANNA PETROVNA, LYUBOV *and* VERA *go into the cubicles.* BESSMERTNY *appears.*)

BESSMERTNY: Is this the famous Kyle? Very interesting. I've just found a contradiction in one of his articles, as it happens.

PTITSYNA: You can start a discussion. Show him how well-educated our patients are.

BESSMERTNY: I'm not joking.

PTITSYNA: Nor am I. There's an age-old notion that we Russians always have to learn from someone else. The French, the Germans, the English, the Americans . . .

BESSMERTNY: They said on the radio that Kyle was bringing some drugs with him—almost half a million dollars' worth!

PTITSYNA: Thanks for nothing. Oh, I'm not talking about Kyle. They'll offer us various decontaminants and medicines. We'll buy them, of course, and they'll wait to see how they work on us. They'll try them out on us, experiment on us like guinea pigs.

BESSMERTNY: Aren't you taking too grim a view?

PTITSYNA: Grumbling, am I? Maybe I am. But I'm fed up that they're using us. And not for the first time. Right now they're making a terrible fuss because the Russians haven't given out any information about the accident. They won't buy our food. They've banned our ships and airplanes from going to their countries because they claim they are polluted by radioactivity. If you believe what they say in the West, there's nothing left for us to do but put on a white sheet and walk to the cemetery. But in a few days the fuss will die down, and they'll start asking permission to come to the site of the accident. To gain experience at *our* expense. And we'll wag our tails, grin our heads off and say, "Please come. Delighted to have you. . . ."

BESSMERTNY: Russians are generous by nature.

PTITSYNA: They lecture us and lecture us and we welcome them with open arms.

BESSMERTNY: So it was, is and always shall be! It will never be otherwise. We have more than enough troubles of our own, but we are always weeping over other people's misfortunes. But you're wrong about Kyle. He's come here with his children, after all. Others are taking theirs away, out of Russia, but he's bringing his with him. He's a good man. He takes our grief to heart. And that's worth more than millions.

PTITSYNA: That's true. No doubt I'm suffering from depression too. You see? "Depression"—even here we can't manage without using a foreign word. To put it more simply, what I feel is anguish, incurable anguish. Hollow, boundless, sickening anguish, and there's nowhere to go to escape from it.

BESSMERTNY: Except the usual place—work.

PTITSYNA: You really do know how to console us. Good for you! You've got on your feet again, even though once you were lying there dead drunk. You were living on all fours, like a little dog.

BESSMERTNY: Basically, I've remained one. . . .

PTITSYNA: Now, now, none of that self-pity. You're a hopeless optimist.

(ANNA PETROVNA *comes out of a cubicle.*)

BESSMERTNY: (*Leans towards* PTITSYNA *and whispers to her*) One little question. Is it true what you wrote about me in that article of yours—that the changes in my bone marrow have caused it to lose its individual characteristics?

PTITSYNA: Yes, it is. Why do you want to know?

BESSMERTNY: So my bone marrow is what you'd call absolutely standard, lacking in any special factors?

PTITSYNA: I don't understand you.

BESSMERTNY: And it would be compatible with any other person's?

PTITSYNA: In principle, yes.

BESSMERTNY: Thank you for the information. I'm going back

to my den now. One should be properly prepared to meet our distinguished foreign visitor.

ANNA PETROVNA: Only this time without the hat and the bow tie.

BESSMERTNY: I know what's required. Simple, elegant, dignified. After all, I'm the ace of trumps in your hand.

PTITSYNA: My dear boy, I don't know what we'd have done without you!

BESSMERTNY: I won't wear a hat and bow tie, and you will stop calling me "my dear boy." Agreed? Just "comrade" or, because this is an international occasion, "Mr. Bessmertny."

(*He goes into his cubicle.*)

PTITSYNA: How are things in there?

ANNA PETROVNA: The picture as before, unfortunately. Obviously, with such high doses our treatment procedures are not very effective. They're a little better, but only just . . .

PTITSYNA: When we began, we couldn't even save them when they'd had four hundred. Now we're managing it with doses of more than six hundred. People who used to spend months here and didn't always get out alive are now in ordinary clinics. And you say "only just." Of course one would like to move faster, but radiation sickness is an appalling disease. It'll be more of a scourge than cancer.

ANNA PETROVNA: I realize that, but inwardly I can't accept it. I keep resisting the thought.

PTITSYNA: I remember you when you were quite a young girl doing your internship, like Vera and Lyubov. You wanted to run away. You went through agonies and you didn't believe . . .

ANNA PETROVNA: They're good girls, both of them.

PTITSYNA: We'll take them on here. For a start, I'll get residence permits and rooms for them. They've been through the very worst. They'll turn out well in time.

(*Enter* SERGEYEV *and* PROFESSOR KYLE.)

SERGEYEV: And this is our third floor—the section you've heard about and that you wanted to see. Allow me to introduce you. This is Professor Ptitsyna and this is Professor—

ANNA PETROVNA: Doctor.

SERGEYEV: Dear Anna Petrovna, modest as ever.

KYLE: Very glad to meet you.

SERGEYEV: (*Indicating* VERA *and* LYUBOV) And these young ladies are our interns. As I was telling you, the Institute always takes in a number of doctors who normally practice at atomic power stations and at clinics specializing in radiobiology. They spend some time working in our laboratories to familiarize themselves with the latest research, just as they do in your country.

KYLE: Oh, yes. The system we've developed in our centers is designed to correspond as nearly as possible to the interests of the patients. After all, it's them we are working for—all of us are, aren't we?

SERGEYEV: Of course. I've seen some of your specialized clinics. Ideal.

PTITSYNA: We had them first, by the way.

KYLE: Unfortunately, information about your experience is

not always widely distributed. One of the objects of my trip is to bring American and European public opinion up to date on the real state of affairs here. Let me say at once, your information fully corresponds to reality, but we in the West are used to something different. Forgive a critical observation, but I was told that with you criticism is now in fashion. Isn't that so?

PTITSYNA: The fact that your public is badly informed is not our fault but your misfortune.

SERGEYEV: Lydia Stepanovna!

PTITSYNA: I'll keep silent.

KYLE: Oh come now, Professor. You're right, without a doubt. I regularly publish your excellent papers in my own journal. Unfortunately, over the last two or three years I haven't seen so many of them, but each one of them is a pearl.

PTITSYNA: I'm getting old, and so I am ill more often. And I'm too lazy to write much these days.

KYLE: Oh, that's so sad, Professor! Your experience and your knowledge are priceless. Believe me, I've always sincerely regretted not seeing you at our congresses and conferences. I've so often invited you to come.

PTITSYNA: Please don't take it amiss. I'm rather a stay-at-home.

KYLE: Professor Sergeyev comes regularly. And he always makes brilliant contributions.

SERGEYEV: Thank you. May I show you . . . ? (*Gestures towards Cubicle No. 1*) Unfortunately, some of our patients . . .

KYLE: I understand. You have my profound sympathy. I've seen the state of affairs in other clinics. What has happened is terrible, but your excellent specialists are doing everything possible. I've appealed to world public opinion, and I think that all necessary aid will be forthcoming. You probably know that I have donated medicines to the value of half a million dollars. That's just the first contribution. Our aid may eventually be more significant. I'm ready.

(SERGEYEV *and* KYLE *go into Cubicle No. 1.*)

ANNA PETROVNA: (*To* PTITSYNA) Why do you have to argue with him?

PTITSYNA: It's my bad character coming out. I've never learned to keep my tongue in check.

VERA: He's not bad, that American professor. Well turned out.

LYUBOV: They know how to look after themselves.

PTITSYNA: No need to be petty. He really is a first-class specialist, but . . .

(SERGEYEV *and* KYLE *go into the next cubicle.*)

ANNA PETROVNA: But what?

PTITSYNA: He's a magnificent surgeon, but bone-marrow transplants is only of any help at certain dosages of radiation. If the dose is a little more than six hundred, it's useless. He thinks transplantation is a panacea.

ANNA PETROVNA: A marrow specialist. They're all like that.

(SERGEYEV *and* KYLE *come out of the cubicle. The American is shaking his head sadly. They go into the next cubicle.*)

LYUBOV: Do they have institutes like this one in America?

PTITSYNA: I doubt it. It's too expensive to maintain if there aren't enough patients. And they know how to count the pennies.

(SERGEYEV *and* KYLE *come out, then proceed to the next cubicle.*)

ANNA PETROVNA: I think they'll have to start having them now. This is the atomic age, after all.

PTITSYNA: They'll look and see how we do it. They'll do the same, call in the journalists, who will write about the marvelous new clinic, and then they'll come over here and say that *we* have been copying them.

VERA: You sound as if you thought the Russians invented the wheel, the steam engine, the motor car and the airplane.

PTITSYNA: No, we didn't invent all those things. But in radiobiology we are ahead, that's for sure. And you'll see how he reacts when he realizes it.

(SERGEYEV *and* KYLE *go into* BESSMERTNY's *cubicle.*)

This will amuse the dear boy! Kyle will relieve his boredom for a while. (*To* ANNA PETROVNA) Was it you who told him about his bone marrow?

ANNA PETROVNA: He knows it all anyway. He's the inquisitive sort.

PTITSYNA: I didn't like his mood when he was talking to me just now.

(SERGEYEV, KYLE *and* BESSMERTNY *come out of the cubicle.*)

BESSMERTNY: (*Handing* KYLE *a medical journal*) There you are, Mr. Kyle. My case has been written up in here. In the greatest detail. I can hardly add anything to it.

KYLE: Thank you. I'm most grateful. You're a remarkable patient.

SERGEYEV: He likes playing the eccentric!

BESSMERTNY: No. I just wanted a chat with Mr. Kyle about various global problems. My personal fate is no more than a grain of sand in a storm that rages over the entire planet.

KYLE: You have described the situation very accurately, Mr. . . .

BESSMERTNY: Bessmertny.

KYLE: Yes, of course, Bessmertny. And visiting your clinic has made me even more certain of it.

VERA: Do you have research like this in America?

KYLE: Not yet. But I'm now firmly persuaded that it is absolutely necessary. And Mr. . . . Bessmertny has convinced me of it. That's a funny surname you have.

BESSMERTNY: It's a pseudonym. Like Stendhal or George Sand. I don't recall any American who used a pseudonym. But that's neither here nor there.

KYLE: Quite so. And I'm completely shattered by what I've seen here. It's fantastic.

PTITSYNA: Yes, the radiation doses really are fantastic.

KYLE: I agree with you, Professor Ptitsyna. It is a terrible tragedy, and we must draw from it all the lessons we can. The experience you've gained from your treatment of these cases is amazing. I imagined that with doses of this magnitude the prognosis would be instant and fatal. Yet you have achieved astounding results.

SERGEYEV: Your assessment of our work is very flattering, Professor. We are grateful for it.

KYLE: I'm giving a press conference tomorrow. I should like you, Professor Sergeyev, and you, Professor Ptitsyna, to be alongside me when the journalists start attacking me.

PTITSYNA: I can't. I'll be working.

KYLE: I quite understand. But you, Professor, simply must be with me. I have got to show the press what superb specialists are working in your country. I must do that.

SERGEYEV: Thank you. I'll be there.

KYLE: The most important thing that you and I must bring home to the world press is that this tragedy at the nuclear power station is a minor incident compared with a nuclear war. We have now had a vivid illustration of what it can be like.

VERA: But you in America . . .

SERGEYEV: Vera!

KYLE: I quite understand what my young colleague was about to say. Yes, we do have different views and different interpretations of events, but I think we doctors are united in one thing: in the case of a nuclear catastrophe, no one would get treated. There simply aren't enough of us doctors. It will mean universal destruction and death.

BESSMERTNY: A sarcophagus.

KYLE: What? I don't quite understand.

BESSMERTNY: A collective, universal sarcophagus.

KYLE: Perfect. Have I your permission to use that simile?

BESSMERTNY: You have. I don't mind at all. . . .

KYLE: I'd like to tell the world about you, your sense of humor, your unique case history. Of course I can't invite you to America. I realize that's impossible, but . . .

BESSMERTNY: It's awfully far away and I don't like flying. Supposing the plane crashed?

KYLE: (*Laughs*) That's good! I like you Russians so much—even at the worst moments you can always make a joke!

BESSMERTNY: (*Grimly*) Yes, it really is very funny.

(*The lights in Cubicles No. 1 and No. 8 start to blink, and the buzzer is heard from the console.*)

PTITSYNA: Excuse me, we have to . . .

KYLE: I won't keep you. Goodbye and thank you.

SERGEYEV: I'll see you out.

BESSMERTNY: (*To* KYLE) One minute, Professor. I'd like a word with you as one plain man to another. Without any formality or diplomacy. OK? Forget that you're an American among Russians. Tell me honestly—are you appalled by all this? (*Points to the cubicles.*)

KYLE: (*Perplexed*) Very much . . . It's hard to believe that such a thing could . . .

BESSMERTNY: Well, when you're back in America, tell your people—the ones with their fingers on the button—that if they ever press it, there'll be nothing left, nothing. Or only people like me. And take it from me, there is no life and no joy in my existence. Tell them that.

KYLE: I certainly will.

BESSMERTNY: You're a good man, Mr. Kyle. Pity about our new "dry" law—I'd have liked to split a bottle of vodka with you. All the best, Professor. I wish you a long and happy life!

(*Exeunt* KYLE *and* SERGEYEV. PTITSYNA *and* VERA, ANNA PETROVNA *and* LYUBOV *go into Cubicles No. 1 and No. 8.*)

(*Thoughtfully*) Full stop. I seem to have achieved world fame at last . . .

(*The light goes out in Cubicle No. 1.* PTITSYNA *comes out.*)

Lydia Stepanovna, can I talk to you seriously for a moment?

PTITSYNA: Is it so urgent?

BESSMERTNY: Yes. Do you remember after my first operation you said to me, "Ask whatever you want and I'll do it for you"?

PTITSYNA: I did say something of the sort.

BESSMERTNY: I want to ask that of you now.

PTITSYNA: After such a long wait?

BESSMERTNY: The time has come. Take some of my bone marrow and give it to the man in No. 5.

PTITSYNA: What are you saying, my dear boy!

BESSMERTNY: I'm serious.

PTITSYNA: It's an enormous risk. For you. I haven't the right.

BESSMERTNY: It's at *my* request, so you have the right. It's got to be done.

PTITSYNA: Calm down . . .

BESSMERTNY: I am quite calm and in my right mind—perhaps for the first time in all these 488 days. I have a right, at least once in my life, to do something meaningful. For the first time in my life . . .

PTITSYNA: You shouldn't, you know. . . .

(ANNA PETROVNA *comes out of Cubicle No. 5.*)

BESSMERTNY: Yes, I should. Bessmertny? "The Immortal"? Ridiculous. I'm no immortal, I'm a rabbit. And I always was. Life? As a rabbit? Of course, I can cope with it, and I'll stay as a rabbit, but on one condition. I must save him. (*Points to Cubicle No. 5.*)

ANNA PETROVNA: Why him?

BESSMERTNY: He must live. He has no right to die along with them. (*Points to the other cubicles.*) Remember how it was in the Middle Ages? A leper had a bell hung round his neck, so that when he walked around the town everyone knew that a leper was coming. Today everyone needs to know and to see that one of the guilty ones is coming. Let them point the finger at him. Let them frighten their children with the sight of him. I would print his portrait on the front page of every newspaper. I would use him as an example for schoolchildren, to show what they should *not* grow up into. I would take him from town to town and show him to people: "There he is! Look, one of the chief culprits!" I want to condemn him to life. . . .

(The lights in all the cubicles, except No. 5, slowly go out. PTITSYNA *embraces* BESSMERTNY *and goes with him into Cubicle No. 10. The telephone rings.* ANNA PETROVNA *picks up the receiver.)*

ANNA PETROVNA: Hullo . . . Lev Ivanovich, yes . . . I see . . . in an hour's time? We'll be ready. . . . *(Replaces receiver. To* VERA *and* LYUBOV) Another six patients. They'll be bringing them soon. We must get the cubicles ready.

(Exeunt. The glow on the cyclorama starts to fade. The light in Cubicle No. 10 is slowly extinguished.)

MALE VOICE ON RADIO: Here is an announcement from the cast, the director and the author. "This play is dedicated to Pravik, Lelechinenko, Kibenko and Ignatenko, Tishchura and Vashuk, Titenko and Telyatnikov, Busygin and Gritsenko; the firemen and power-station workers, the physicists and calibrators, the officers, helicopter pilots and miners, adults and children; to all those who, at the cost of their lives and health, extinguished the nuclear flames of Chernobyl."

(The glow of the cyclorama fades out. The stage is dark except for the light flashing in Cubicle No. 5.)

THE CURTAIN SLOWLY DESCENDS.

ABOUT THE AUTHOR

Vladimir Gubaryev was born in 1938 in Mogilev. An engineer by training, he joined *Pravda* in 1976 as a science correspondent and then as science editor. He has written over twenty books on space flight and the use of atomic energy, including his unique survey of space travel, *The Space Age*. He has visited major scientific centers throughout the world and was the first journalist to cover controlled nuclear explosions, which he described in his book *Two Paces from the Epicenter*. He has also scripted a number of documentary films and a feature film, *The Ship of Newcomers*, which was produced by the Gorky Studios in 1986.

Vladimir Gubaryev is the author of four plays. Two of these, *Let's Go!* and *Special Flight*, have been performed in several Soviet theaters. After the accident at the Chernobyl nuclear power station he was the first journalist on the scene and the first to report on it in *Pravda*. He followed this series of articles by his play *Sarcophagus*, which he wrote in July 1986.

Vladimir Gubaryev is a member of the USSR Union of Writers and a winner of the USSR State Prize and of numerous other awards, including the Lenin Komsomol Prize.